ADULT LITERACY IN A NEW ERA

Dear Stephen

Thank you!

Thank you!

Thank you!

with much
warmth,
Jeannine

ADULT LITERACY IN A NEW ERA
Reflections from the Open Book

Dianne Ramdeholl

Paradigm Publishers
Boulder • London

To the students
of the Open Book

Copyright © 2011 by Paradigm Publishers

Published in the United States by Paradigm Publishers, 2845 Wilderness Place, Boulder, Colorado 80301 USA.

Paradigm Publishers is the trade name of Birkenkamp & Company, LLC, Dean Birkenkamp, President and Publisher.

Library of Congress Cataloging-in-Publication Data

Ramdeholl, Dianne.
 Adult literacy in a new era : reflections from the Open Book / Dianne Ramdeholl.
  p. cm.
 Includes bibliographical references.
 ISBN 978-1-59451-848-5 (hardcover : alk. paper) — ISBN 978-1-59451-849-2 (pbk. : alk. paper)
  1. Adult education—United States.   2. Functional literacy—United States.
3. Literacy—United States.   4. Literacy programs—Evaluation.   I. Title.
 LC5251.R36 2011
 374'.973—dc23   2011018152

Printed and bound in the United States of America on acid-free paper that meets the standards of the American National Standard for Permanence of Paper for Printed Library Materials.

Designed and Typeset by Straight Creek Bookmakers.

15 14 13 12 11   5 4 3 2 1

Contents

Setting the Context

> In New York City, 1.6 million people do not have their GED and nearly a third of all adults are below the average adult literacy level. In the United States, 30 million people over age sixteen—14 percent of the country's adult population—don't read well enough to understand a newspaper story written at the eighth-grade level or fill out a job application.
> —National Assessment of Adult Literacy, 2003

Research clearly demonstrates that adult illiteracy is an enormously pervasive issue in the United States, and adults who aren't literate lack adequate access to basic resources and social supports (Comings and Soricone, 2007; Prins, Toso, and Schafft, 2008; Purcell-Gates and Waterman, 2000). Although millions of adults participate in adult literacy programs, there are very few current studies that document aspects of the adult literacy field's history and practices—and even fewer studies that situate that narrative within a liberating paradigm. Many researchers (McLaren, 1998; Rivera, 2008; Allman, 2010) have called for rethinking how adult literacy education is framed in this country. This oral history study, chronicling the history of a grassroots, adult, community-based program, is an effort to do that by contributing to a larger collective dialogue.

Though many adults come to literacy programs still struggling to overcome profound feelings of inadequacy and marginalization (as well as other barriers based on prior school experiences), adult literacy education can represent a site of significant transformation. It is only through listening to stories from a field cloaked in invisibility that practices rooted in education for democratic social change can be highlighted (Allman, 2010; Slim and Thompson, 1995; Nadeau, 1996; Torres, 1995).

This book, an oral history study, explores the story of one literacy program in Brooklyn, New York, that was rooted in democratic principles and shared decision-making. At present, adult literacy education is replicating the K–12 system, an industrialized factory model that has been (and continues to be) unsuccessful for entire communities. As in the K–12 system, student success is defined mainly by standardized assessments. In adult literacy programs, the National Reporting System (NRS)—which is part of the Workforce Investment Act (WIA), the main federal funding source for adult literacy programs in the United States—currently defines student success solely by standardized test scores (Comings and Soricone, 2007; Prins, 2008; Sparks and Peterson, 2000). Heaney (2007) states that adult literacy in this country has been reduced to a technical problem in need of a technical solution. Through operationalizing adult literacy, there is no space for community empowerment models that have the potential to foster sustainable change by redistributing power in equitable ways. Instead, the oppressive structures of government funding (which most adult literacy programs in New York, including the Open Book, survive on) contribute to programs' further marginalization and invisibility. Government funding was never intended to fund social justice movements that could support widespread social change. To be clear, in this climate, literacy programs dance to the funders' song, and that song will never be social change. Instead of addressing deep institutionalized inequities and the needs of marginalized communities, government funding, which is ludicrously inadequate, does little more than make cosmetic adjustments to give dominant culture the appearance of progressivism. The funds really keep systems of oppression and exploitation intact. In such a climate it is therefore unsurprising that the program this book is based on was not sustainable. The importance of research and practices that place students' interests, concerns, and lives at the center of their education process is paramount, yet continues to be diminished (Auerbach, 1992; Heaney, 1996; Luttrell, 1997).

This book also examines the ways in which adult literacy students and teachers at the Open Book redefined and renegotiated their identities both inside and outside the classroom, reconstructed human agency, and in the process became more powerful people. Given the dire economic climate in this country, the education of adults is ever more important. Nadeau (1996) says studies that preserve collective historical memory help to affirm both who we are and who we might become. Yet, the public historical memory of adult literacy is being rewritten minus any connections to a democratic, just world. The story you're about to read is, in essence, an effort to subvert that direction by exploring democratic possibilities through shared decision-making at an adult literacy program. However, it would be naïve (even irresponsible) not to explicitly state how difficult it is to contest the measures that dominate education and the ways in which this dominance is inextricably tied into larger entrenched issues and structures. Adult education can subvert, through deep analysis, structures in our society that support this injustice and dehumanization. Deep understanding of these structures and the ways they affect adult literacy is the first step toward any possible dismantlement of these oppressive systems.

Bannerji (2005) points out ways in which spheres of the economic, political, and cultural are ontologically inseparable. She discusses the powerful effects of discourse on lived experience and also how race and class establish difference and find long-lasting ways of reproducing this practice of inequity. This creates normalized and experiential knowledge about whose labor counts the least (and can therefore be exploited the most). It is to this invisible and exploited group that the majority of adult literacy students belong.

From this perspective, the role of literacy in social relations becomes clearer. Freire (1970) states the solution is not to integrate people into current structures of oppression but to transform those structures so they can become more humane versions of themselves. Graff (1987) has shown that the purpose of education isn't to provide reading and writing of words and worlds but instead to train people to a new work discipline, permeated with middle-class obsession of morality and character. A Marxist perspective provides tools for analyzing the socioeconomic context in which illiteracy has a role. Alden (1982) also posits that this perspective leads to a clearer understanding of the actions of those belonging to the dominant culture, many of whose businesses and industries rely on cheap labor of the poor and poorly educated.

Yet, the vast majority of publicly funded adult literacy research continues to be focused on the numerical. Most programs in New York City that receive public funding through the Workforce Investment Act Title 2 are forced to accept gains on standardized tests as the only legitimate marker of student progress. This reductionistic culture that solely privileges test scores has had a devastating impact on adult literacy policy, practice, and discourse. It has largely succeeded in transforming rather than representing what literacy means in these economies. With rigid measurements, the landscape of adult literacy has been inextricably altered, with programs having to focus on reading, writing, and numeracy skills imposed by groups with other agendas and interests. Hautecoeur (1997) has pointed out that, during the 1990s, most industrialized nations "made Draconian cuts in adult education, seeing basic education as providing vocational qualifications and employability training."

Adult literacy practitioners feel this tension every day, where they come face-to-face with the dissonance between what adult students want to learn and what policy says they should learn. In this environment, students who have been marginalized by a school system are further oppressed because literacy is being used as an effective weapon to shift further blame onto poor communities of color (instead of recognizing the more complex historical contexts of unequal distribution of resources). Macedo (1994) says that only by engaging in pedagogies of resistance may we be able to reclaim adult literacy's roots and foster sustainable spaces driven by social justice interests.

At its core, the oral history study of the Open Book represents a counter-narrative, a critique of dominant culture. Freire (1970) called for people to interrupt dominant scripts and rewrite roadmaps of power. The Open Book attempted to do precisely this. Boggs (1998) reminds us that as members of this society we must leap to new stages of becoming more *human* human beings. Recognizing the damage that a highly developed capitalist system has inflicted on the humanity of its members, we as a society must make a commitment to create strategies to transform ourselves into more human human beings—a struggle not only against the external enemy but also the enemy within (Boggs, 1998, pp. 151–152). In this and other oral histories, people tell their own stories to become actors in a historical script that they themselves author. In this act, they become knowledge producers. When we honor people's stories, we become world travelers. We learn to live in each other's countries, speak each other's languages, negotiate each other's streets, and turn our keys into each other's locks (Blaise, 1993).

The Open Book was, above all else, an effort to support student leadership: a quest for agency and equity through shared governance and solidarity. Like democratic practice, student leadership involves being able to reimagine and move beyond fixed definitions or frameworks to renegotiate and re-envision new alternatives.

Calvin Miles worked on developing student leadership at the Open Book and was a powerful student leader in New York City and the board president of VALUE (Voices for Adult Literacy United to Educate, the only national organization for adult learners in the United States). He says the following about adult literacy in New York City.

> I think if the Open Book was open today, you would have had one of the strongest groups coming out of that school. I thought they were on the right track of developing strong student leadership. It just felt good when you went to that program. I felt like I could do anything I wanted to do there.

One thing we have not done is help students to organize other students. We have to be able to let students figure this stuff out for themselves. Students can communicate with students much better than teachers.

The civil rights movement didn't start with everybody involved. It started on a small scale and worked its way to everybody. We need an adult literacy movement in this country. We need to say that we are not going to accept [the government] giving little dabs of money. You need to give us money before we can be able to do the things we are doing. Right now we're not seen as valuable. We're seen as failures. That's got to change. More students need to be leaders, and they need to tell their stories. Programs have to trust students. Program directors should not think students are trying to destroy the program. One of the worst things in the field now is that students are not talking to each other. The literacy community needs to get together and work better together. Right now we're not working the system; the system is working us. We got folks that don't know nothing about the field telling us what we should be doing and it's not fair. We should take the field back. As long as I'm living, I'll be fighting for this cause.

*   *   *

Tragically, Calvin died on January 22, 2009. Calvin clearly believed, however, that we must overcome our cultural aversion toward entire segments of our society. We must challenge notions of imperialism in our struggle toward justice for everyone. As adult literacy workers, we must make space for fragile democratic efforts and experiments that can foster human agency. We need to ask ourselves to what extent can we collectively disentangle and disengage our current ways of being and living in the world, while learning to open windows in our psyches that honor collective responsibility and humane, democratic possibilities. It's clear from the story of the Open Book that we must find ways to listen to what students have to say and incorporate those words, dreams, hopes, and desires into the tapestry of adult literacy programs (and society). Freire (1970) points out that without true dialogue, a faith in people's power to make and remake, to create and re-create, to become more fully human becomes nearly impossible.

Over the years, many have articulated the notion that Freire's most deeply held vision for the future—the creation of a world in which it would be easier to love—is impossible as long as institutionalized inequities continue to thrive.

Adult education has a pivotal role to play in preparing people to challenge unjust socioeconomic systems that increasingly dominate the lives of the vast majority of human beings and rob us of humanity by dehumanizing entire subsections of society, fragmenting our sense of responsibility for one another and the world we inhabit. Maxine Greene (personal communication, 2003) says that we must learn to live and labor in the spaces and possibilities between freedom and imagination—to make present what is absent, to summon up a condition that is not yet.

Foreword

John Gordon

We were each other's heroes.

—Antonia Bueno, Open Book student

With five words, Antonia gives voice, eloquently and profoundly, to one of the central notions of the Open Book: that the critical dialogues and relationships in adult education are as much among students as between students and teachers; that everyone, students and teachers alike, brings important ideas and experience to the classroom; that everyone in the room is a teacher. Implicit in this idea is a critique of "traditional" conceptions of the student-teacher relationship (of the teacher as "knower" and the student as "learner"), a critique that goes well beyond demanding recognition of student voices. Implicit as well is a sense that the promise of adult education, like all education worthy of the name, is in its potential for transformation.

While these ideas enjoyed a certain currency in some sectors of the adult education field, particularly in the late 1980s, by the 1990s, as welfare reform and the Workforce Investment Act reshaped the field, few people were really thinking of adult education in those terms.

The Open Book was founded in 1985, in the wave of new programs started with funding saved after the banks took control of New York City's finances during the 1975 fiscal crisis, slashing the budget and imposing policies that led to massive layoffs and the dismantling of social service infrastructures. Good Shepherd Services, a local agency doing work primarily with children and families, had submitted a proposal to the city the previous summer. In an act that seemed foolhardy to me even then, they hired me—an activist with no real teaching experience—as the teacher-coordinator. Good Shepherd had acquired some temporary space in the basement of a Catholic elementary school around the corner; I had done some reading, visited a few literacy classes at New York City Technical College, and developed some rudimentary plans for teaching. The Open Book began classes on January 2, 1985, one week after I started.

We began with a pretty broad and vague mission, which I scribbled out on a piece of notebook paper several months later in response to a prompt from the part-time teacher working with the evening group:

"The Open Book is a place where people from the community can come and learn the kinds of things they feel they need to learn in order to improve their lives, their families, and their community."

The mission made sense to me, and I think I understood that framing it in terms of what people wanted to learn, rather than what we or I thought they needed to learn, challenged the mainstream notion that literacy was all or only about developing a technical skill (reading) or getting a general equivalency diploma (GED). But I really didn't have a very elaborate notion of what that mission meant or what it would look like in practice. Over time I kept coming back to it, thinking we needed to develop something more, but I didn't know what that would be. I think now that the very simplicity of the mission was its strength.

One month later, I hired Cecilia Weinraub, a woman from the neighborhood who had just gotten her GED after completing a displaced homemaker program run by Good Shepherd, as a part-time program assistant. This proved to be a key decision. Cecilia had grown up in Venezuela and had only gone to the third grade. From then on she had run the streets. A voracious and wide-ranging reader, she was completely self-taught and had read at least as widely as any of the teachers had—from Dostoevsky to Greek mythology to African history. Her writing skills were weak and I don't think she had ever filed anything in her life. But Cecilia brought a deep and nuanced understanding of the community we were hoping to serve, a counterpoint to the theoretical perspective that I and later on other teachers brought to our work. She believed strongly in the Open Book's mission, helped to shape it into something concrete, and never hesitated to challenge the other teachers and staff to live up to it. She, more than anyone, grounded us in the community and kept us real. A few years later, when some new funding was made available, Cecilia became our first counselor.

The New York City adult literacy community was, in a sense, wide open. While the new funding was certainly driven by workforce development concerns, the expansion of programs brought lots of new people into the field, many of them attracted by a sense of the potential of adult literacy to be a site for social change. There was plenty of room for experimentation, and teachers were pushing the boundaries of existing pedagogy that seemed to many of us to be rooted in paternalistic and narrow conceptions of literacy.

We went to conferences, visited other programs, and read everything we could get our hands on. Like many in the field, we had come in without much theoretical background. Over time, we began to acquire some of that, but in many ways our inexperience was a plus. We may not have known that much about teaching, but we had the good sense to know when we should step back and let people talk. And very soon, our classroom became a place that was about a lot more than reading and writing. Students began talking about what was going on in their lives. They began telling (and writing) their stories. In time, their stories moved from the margins of the class to its center.

From the beginning we opened up questions about curriculum to students. And we began to bring the classes together once a month or so in community meetings. That first summer, we moved up the block to our own space, and students came together to paint the classrooms. That seemed natural at the time, but, looking back, it feels like a defining moment: students actively asserting their deep connection with the school.

The following year, Basemah Jaber showed up at the Open Book. A Palestinian activist and survivor of domestic violence, Basemah came into our beginning reading class and quickly established a presence. She pushed the teachers to open up the decision-making process and encouraged her fellow students to take leadership and speak up for what they wanted. She actively contributed during class, planned meetings, and tirelessly organized student participation. Outside of the school, Basemah also began to organize groups for Arabic women who were dealing with issues of domestic violence. Soon, she was bringing those groups into the Open Book, meeting with them in our library. When Basemah advanced into our next-level class, she became an assistant teacher, working with the beginning class two days a week. She was a founding member of Adult United Voices, a citywide student group that advocated for more student involvement in their programs.

Many amazing students followed, and slowly the Open Book developed into a school with strong student involvement and leadership. That story is told in the pages that follow, assembled in loving and painstaking detail by Dianne Ramdeholl. It involved important choices by teachers like Stephanie Lawson, who taped and transcribed the first group of oral histories, and Virginia Naughton, who brought a naturalistic and nonjudgmental style into the room. But the real engine of the Open Book's development was the students, who took the opportunities they had and made the Open Book their own, who developed a sense of family, and who consistently articulated a theory of learning that revolved around notions of family and community.

Of course, this mission, this sense of the Open Book as first and foremost a community, a place where people could develop the skills they felt they needed, was not the purpose of the funding. The Open Book's development was shaped by the larger context in which we were operating. We often found ourselves at odds with forces and institutions outside us. In particular:

1. The neighborhood we were operating in was suffering through an intense wave of gentrification that would ultimately drive most of our students out of the immediate area. This process became an important focus of our curriculum in the early years. Ironically, it also resulted in a broadening of our student body, which was at that time primarily Puerto Rican. As time went on, more and more black students, both African American and Afro-Caribbean, came to the Open Book.

2. As the Open Book matured, many of our students who were on public assistance faced increasing pressure to leave the school and participate in workfare. Again, this became an important focus of classroom and school-wide dialogue. It also led us into a struggle with the city agencies that oversaw public assistance.

3. The fact that we were a program of a social service agency that received the vast majority of its funding from government sources and focused primarily on children and family services led to tensions with our parent organization.

4. The particular shape of education funding, with its focus on testing, GEDs, and employment, came into conflict with our commitment to our mission—in particular, our commitment to participatory education, community, and student-driven programming. This was especially true after the passage of the Workforce Investment Act in 1998.

Ultimately, these contradictions probably strengthened the Open Book. We all struggled to understand what was going on around us, and we were forced to define what was important about the way we were working and what we were willing to fight for. The Open Book inspired a tremendous amount of loyalty and love. When Dianne began this project, the response was overwhelming; she stopped recording stories not because she ran out of people who wanted to be interviewed, but because documenting the multiple stories (and the countless other stories nestled within those stories) in all their complexity could have continued indefinitely.

Before inviting you to read on, I want to conclude with a moment closer to the end of the Open Book than the beginning. We were in the habit of organizing a school picnic in Prospect Park at the end of every school year. This particular year, as we came close to the end of June, it somehow became known that Kanak, a longtime student, had always wanted to learn to ride a bike. Placed in an arranged marriage when she was fourteen years old, Kanak immigrated to the United States with her husband's family as a young woman. Relegated to a role of cooking and cleaning for the family, she came to the Open Book in the hopes of earning her high school diploma. Kanak came faithfully to class and spent hours afterward every day studying and working on her computer skills. Her struggle to define her own destiny was at the center of her writing as well as a lot of her conversations with fellow students and teachers, and she inspired us with her tenacity and courage. Learning to ride a bike, of course, was about many things beyond simple transportation. It would bring a measure of independence and symbolized, perhaps, overcoming all those forces that had kept her down throughout her life. And as anyone who rides a bike knows, it represented freedom and joy.

Well, the day came, hot and sunny. Many students were there with their families and friends, and we were all crowded around the barbecue, talking and laughing. Antonia and Kanak set off down one of the park paths by themselves with a borrowed bike, Kanak astride the bicycle and Antonia running alongside and holding on. Twenty minutes later they were back, Kanak atop the saddle, riding freely, triumphant; Antonia walking behind, a huge smile on her face.

We were each other's heroes.

Preface

I walked quietly into the classroom and took a seat. I usually sat at the back of each classroom, whenever possible, in a mostly futile attempt at minimal intrusion. In my role, part of my responsibility was to visit different literacy programs around New York City (NYC), sit in on classes, and talk with instructors, program directors, and students.

Invariably, instructors in almost every class I visited would be sitting at the front of the room (with students sitting in rows) instructing students to open their workbooks to a certain page, read a decontextualized passage silently, and answer the multiple-choice questions. This directive was often met with silence, followed with students lowering their heads. A few students might begin working independently. I often heard students mutter sentiments such as "This is too hard." "Too boring." Often I heard sounds of exaggerated yawns. In one particular class I was sitting in, I looked over at the instructor. He was sitting at his desk, head lowered, seemingly immersed in his own paperwork. He briefly looked up. "We're going over this in a few minutes." I went over and asked for a copy of the reading that students were currently assigned to. It happened to be an article about the upcoming marathon in NYC. I wondered whether students had requested learning about this. Was one of them participating in the marathon? Did they know someone who was? Was this reading contextualized as part of a larger theme or unit? Though I was reluctant to rush to judgment, I could feel parts of myself already doing so. Where were students' voices reflected in this activity? Had they specifically requested this? I again looked around the room. I saw the bare walls, cracked and chipped, pleading for at least one fresh coat of paint. Many of the students in that particular class seemed plastered into the too small seats their grown-up bodies were squeezed into; a vaguely embarrassed air floated around the room, although this could have only been my imagination. On that day, there were two students who seemed to be having obvious difficulty with the text. They kept opening and closing their dictionaries. Four other students had given up any pretense of engaging with the text and instead were having a spirited discussion in their definition of hushed tones about an incident in last week's class.

After fifteen minutes, the instructor went around the room asking each student to read one of the questions and her answer. I noticed the two students who seemed to be struggling earlier were having great difficulty even reading their answers. How much did they understand of the text? Did they have the slightest interest in the marathon? When I later asked the instructor whether they were in the correct level, he told me that was the level assigned to them by the Test for Adult Basic Education (TABE), the assessment required by funders. What about alternative assessments? Portfolios? Journals? Reflective logs? The instructor shrugged. "I would love to do all of that but I get paid [for] five hours a week. That's how much I teach here. I don't get paid for planning and I certainly wouldn't get paid to read students' journals and writing."

No easy answers, just the bulging, endless need flowing out of programs and onto the streets where people unheedingly trample all over it. It always surprises me that pedestrians can't feel it underfoot, that they don't slip and fall on it. Need ... the overwhelming kind that leaves you hollow and breathless with its scope and depth. Need for more funding, for different adult literacy policy, for students' voices and perspectives to be included in decision-making, for different visions and models of instruction, for more instructors, for more students to be served by more programs, for more quality, for more resistance against the tide. You can scoop it up and feel it; the need is everywhere ... thick and unbearably cold.

On that particular day in that classroom I was in, there was no reading aloud of the text, no discussion or reactions (no possible attempts to engage readers or find ways to link the words in the text to their lives), no predictions about the title, about what could happen next. I asked the instructor about the types of staff development that occurred throughout the year at his agency. "No money, no time," was the answer. He had two other positions teaching in other adult literacy, community-based organizations. Like most of the practitioners in the field, he was just trying to scrape together a living.

After all of the questions related to the text had been answered, the instructor handed out photocopies of another text about the benefits of recycling, which was homework. Audible groans. Crumpling of paper as students hastily put it away and left class in a frantic blur of activity. Several students left their copies on the desk. "See you tomorrow, Professor."

Professor? What was going on there? In community-based organizations I'd worked in, students called instructors by their first name. Students all had and used my home phone number. On birthdays, we would meet after class for group lunches. I don't remember students ever racing out of class. I couldn't imagine that these students and this instructor (a perfectly nice, obviously overworked, exhausted individual) shared any type of closeness. If education involved both the head and the heart, then it seemed both were untouched in this case. Suddenly, without any warning or permission, my mind raced back to an instance in my life when this definitely wasn't so . . . when my heart was so full, it felt like it would burst.

Ten years ago, on a hot and humid day, I walked into a building in a working-class neighborhood in South Brooklyn for an interview as an adult literacy instructor at a community-based agency called the Open Book. I still carefully search my mind as to whether I had some sign, a premonition, that how I perceived the world and my own role in it was about to be forever transformed by that experience, but there were no signs that I can recall.

There were two things I immediately noticed upon entering the classroom for the interview. The first was how airy and filled with sunlight the classroom was; in one corner of the room there were even two large spider plants. This feeling of homey coziness in itself was unusual for community-based organizations (CBOs) due to the constant funding cuts the field faces, which often mean painting and decorating the space isn't possible. Much, much later I learned that Florean, an older student from the South, had walked in one day with the plants and said to the director, "John, I need you to hang these here." Every six months she would come in with new soil and repot the plants. What impact does this action (and many other similar ones by other students) have on creating a space people could call their own?

The second thing I noticed was that there were approximately twelve people sitting around four tables (which were placed together in a rectangle) chatting with each other. The director had mentioned to me earlier that I was going to be interviewed by students, assistant teachers (who were former students), and teachers, so it wasn't a surprise, but the concept was a completely new one to me and somewhat daunting. Yet I felt there was an effort being made to help me feel at ease. Whenever I caught someone's eye, she would smile. Each person had a copy of my résumé and cover letter and everyone in the room had, as part of the hiring committee, studied each prospective candidate's résumé, and, as I later learned, in essence decided (with instructors' support) who would be hired. However, I was completely unaware of any of this as I talked about my teaching practice and underlying beliefs during the interview.

At some point during that conversation it registered in my consciousness that this conversation was very different from other interviews I had been a part of in the past. The questions students asked seemed much more real and rooted in their everyday contexts and lived realities. "I never liked math. I was never good at it. How would you teach the class, knowing this?" Or "Why do you want to work here? What do you think you would bring to this community?" I noticed that while the director and other staff members occasionally asked a question, it seemed fairly clear to me that it was the students who directed the interview. Afterward, I filled out an application in the director's office, and we talked briefly but he seemed interested in getting back to the conversation the hiring committee was involved in regarding the interview I had just participated in.

As I walked toward the elevator, I noticed the new wooden floors and the large windows through which sunlight streamed in on that particular day, but my attention was drawn to the pictures of groups of students that lined the walls. Later I would learn that the program sometimes hired a bus and the students and teachers went to the country for a day. For many of the students it was their first trip out of the city. There were also pieces of student writing arranged neatly on the walls. At a quick glance I noticed poems, reader responses, and essays, all of which seemed to reflect themes from students' lives. It was clear to me that space had been made for students' voices to be heard and that those voices were listened to. The participatory nature aimed at democratizing the place was stamped in so many ways that tiny particles embodying that spirit seemed to float around, inhabiting the very air I breathed. As I made my way out of the building onto the busy street in South Brooklyn where the program was housed, there was a vaguely unsettled feeling lodged in my stomach. I remember the easy, intimate way people joked with each other as well as the obvious affection people shared for one another in the room I'd left not long ago. I had this sense that I had just participated in something powerful, filled with a sense of possibility, but I wasn't sure how. It was as if I had inadvertently stumbled upon something rare, afforded a glimpse into a more hopeful and loving version of education. I felt on the brink of an important discovery but was unable to see or feel any more.

In my ten years of working as an adult literacy practitioner I intuitively felt a difference in the level of community and trust I had just witnessed compared to other literacy programs I had worked. But I couldn't immediately discern what set it apart from those other places. For a moment, I saw a vision of what could be instead of what is. If our classrooms were microcosms of society, then could this program represent an alternative vision, a counterculture, a form of resistance?

However, there was a part of me that rejected this paradigm. Was it really authentic? To what extent were students truly a part of the decision-making process to hire new staff? How much was power really shared between staff and students? Could this program be rooted in an alternative stance critical of the dominant culture and grounded in equity and hope? To what extent was this vision rooted in the collectivity of both students and staff? As a product of this dominant culture and all that it inflicts, I had a lot of unlearning to do. Walking down the street that day, my head swirling with half-formed questions and ideas, I had no idea then of the critical role the Open Book would play in transforming my own philosophy about educational practice and politics and how illusory any separation between the two were.

When the director later told me I was hired, I was both happy and apprehensive. I found myself looking forward to and being afraid of working in a literacy program that was held in exceptionally high regard among the literacy community both in New York and in other states. Because adult literacy is a field that is very much marginalized (not enough funding and the constant threat of yet even more funding cuts) there is inevitably a shadow of vulnerability that looms over the agencies we work in, inevitably fostering angst and worry among both practitioners and students. But somehow I sensed in the pictures and student writing on the walls, in people's voices and the ways they related to each other, that it might be different at this program, and I wanted (needed) to be part of that conversation, that difference, that community in which love and caring and dignity were the cornerstones. I could feel something in my heart beginning to thaw.

Ten years after the day I was hired, the Open Book no longer exists. Hundreds of students and staff have been displaced and devastated by its closing. In this story chronicling the history of the program through participants' voices (the voices that represented that history and reality), some of its power becomes clear through the impressive amount of passion and love that people expressed and that is still clearly stamped in their hearts and consciousness. Over and over participants in this project stressed the importance and urgency of getting this story right because policy-makers and others in the field need to know about this program. The purpose is not to package the "greatness" of the program and export it to the field but instead to contribute to a conversation among students and teachers in other programs to show what's possible within their own programs. It is this collective conversation that we hope will lead to policy changes regarding adult literacy.

On many occasions after interviews, people called me to clarify something they had said, or give an example or anecdote to support their story in the interview. It was evident this experience was very much alive within them and continued to impact their lives in various ways. Several students openly admitted that they couldn't clearly remember their experiences in other literacy programs they had attended but their Open Book experience continued to shape their consciousness. What was it about this program that set it apart from other programs and made it such a unique place where so many people flourished?

In a field that is already disenfranchised, in which students are marginalized, and where powerful stories often ultimately get lost in the rubble of numbers and percentages, we, the co-constructors of this story, believe it is critical to tell this story that is grounded in our everyday struggles and that we believe reflects others' realities in this field. We know that policy preserves and privileges the interests of those in power and doesn't reflect students' voices in meaningful ways, but we believe this must be changed. We hope this book can support that conversation.

While it is almost impossible to condense sixteen years of rich, thick, and textured history in a single document, the collection of conversations chronicling the program's history reflected political struggles students and teachers engaged in, multiple layers of thinking and planning, and the deep love that went into the weaving of the multifaceted tapestry that was the vibrant history of this program. As Cecilia, one of the former counselors from the program, said, "This story you are about to read is like a sand dune: it looks one way in the morning but the wind blows and it shifts during the day, looking entirely different by evening." How it looks depended on whom I spoke with, and whose stories and perspectives were privileged. The story is situated in a moment of magic, filled with possibility, placed between worlds and realities, beyond time and space, where everything resides in a state of fluidity, on slippery slopes of multiple interpretations and understandings, poised for change, for metamorphosis. This story— so far from being over—is still being written by all of us who have been a part of its history, each of us embers waiting to be stoked and fueled; can we together ignite in a new beginning?

Note to the Reader

In the story you're about to read, each chapter (with the exception of the last chapter) is divided into three sections.

- The introduction sets the stage for a conversation.
- The next section is an actual conversation among and by the co-constructors that focuses on events, issues, and themes that were embedded in and representative of the history of the program.
- In the third section, I question, unpack, and problematize the preceding conversations.

For some further insight into how the story took shape and evolved, please see Appendix A. Finally, I would like to point out that people's lives, words, knowledge, love, and commitment shaped both the Open Book and this project. Just as one person isn't a community, this story isn't one person's story. It is our story, our mandate, our dream . . .

—*Dianne Ramdeholl*

Acknowledgments

This book would not have been possible without the support, patience, and faith of many people.

I thank Tom Heaney, Elizabeth Peterson, and Stephen Brookfield—my faculty at National Louis University—for your brilliance and deep generosity of spirit. You were careful and thoughtful guides through the dense forest of stories and theories, teaching me how to merge and live deeply with both.

I would also like to thank the Open Book staff: John Gordon, who has been a true mentor. I will be forever grateful. To others involved in this project: Nancy Hoch, Virginia Naughton, Peggy Conte, Cecilia Weinraub, Stacie Evans, Quisia Gonzalez, Aida Dueno, Yolanda Soto, and Stephanie Lawson. Thank you for believing in and practicing more humane versions of living together in society (and, to that end, envisioning the classroom as a space to rehearse alternative scripts); and for opening your hearts and homes to me with such love. Your kindness and grace will never be forgotten and can never be repaid.

The following exceptional people nourished my soul and tended my fires during this project, and I will forever be grateful to Maura Donnelly, Marlene Haley, Nick Miraflores, Francine Mallozzi, Connie Sommer, and Susan Soggs.

And to Peter Heap for reasons too numerous to mention.

My parents were the first storytellers in my life, creating stories for and with me. They have my eternal love and gratitude for teaching me that courage, integrity, and stories can influence the collective consciousness of society and change the world.

Finally, to the students of the Open Book, this is truly your story. My deepest gratitude for sharing it with me.

—*Dianne Ramdeholl*

ONE

We Are Grains of Sand but Together We Can Make a Beach

The Beginning of the Program

In this book, we, the co-constructors of this story, are opening the collective doors of our hearts and consciousness and invite you to do the same. We want you to enter this story with us, walk into the pages and cover yourselves with the words, breathe them in, touch and taste them—but savor them, reflect on their essence, for they represent our living history of the Open Book. This story, chronicled through our voices, reflects the words of the people who represented and lived that history, that struggle. At times, it seemed as if we entered a portal where we were collectively transported back in time, yet it wasn't really "back" because we were reflecting on the Open Book's powerful impact through each of our lenses, our present experiences, flavored by our current lived realities. It is our hope that this story will support the field in a collective, sustainable conversation rooted in action and change aimed at shifting adult literacy policy in real, meaningful ways. In that vein, we invite you to revise, critique, develop, and add to the perspectives offered.

Since the Open Book closed in 2001, many people in the adult literacy field in New York City continue to question what it was about this program that made it so powerful for so many people. What were the unique elements that separated it from more mainstream adult literacy programs? If it was so successful, why doesn't it still exist? Why don't more programs similar in nature exist? What was it about this place that still continues to impact our lived realities? In these pages, we critically

1

reflect on these and other issues that affected the Open Book, our field, and, most important, the students we served.

It was impossible to condense sixteen years of living history into these pages, to speak with every individual whose heart and life were impacted by the Open Book, who in some way benefited from the culture that was so deeply embedded in the program. Some people have died, others have moved away. And like the sun reflecting off prisms of a rare and precious stone, only certain facets of this program can be highlighted and explored in this story.

The conversation you're about to read takes place among John, Cecilia, and Virginia where they discuss the program in its beginning stages. At this point, eight students had been recruited for the program. Glimpses of the program's emerging philosophy could be seen, even in those very early days. John, the teacher-coordinator of the program for sixteen years, was hired in December 1984. Virginia, one of the first instructors hired, was previously an instructor at Women in Self Help (WISH), another program run by Good Shepherd, the Open Book's umbrella agency. She began by teaching writing at the Open Book one day a week and taught in the program for fifteen years. Cecilia, a graduate of WISH, worked at the program as a counselor for fourteen years. All three of them (like many others) ended up being essential cornerstones upon which the foundation of the program was built.

* * *

John: On a cold January morning, twenty-one years ago, I walked into the basement of a local school and taught the Open Book's first class. A week before, I had been hired as teacher-coordinator. There were about eight or nine students that first day. They were very nervous and not sure what to expect. I was full of ideas, hopes, and visions, but I was also nervous and I didn't know what to expect.... The basement wasn't exactly the best place to hold a class. It was dark and dingy. It had a concrete floor. And we didn't even have a room, just a space in the corner that was separated from the rest of the basement by a row of lockers. Instead of a door, there was an opening between the lockers. We all sat in those old desks that kids use in school. Every fifteen minutes or so, a class of eight-year-olds would be led down into the basement by their teacher to go to the bathroom. The kids would be yelling and laughing. The teacher was usually yelling as well—trying to keep them quiet. It seemed that just about every kid would peek in between the lockers to see what was going on. You can imagine how people felt: nervous and uptight, a little embarrassed because they didn't know how to read well. Most were sitting in a class for the first time in years. It certainly didn't help to have a group of giggling eight-year-olds looking in every fifteen minutes. But we carried on. Pretty soon we got over our nervousness and found that we liked each other. Students began to tell each other their stories, to share what was going on in their lives, to tell about their pain and struggle along with their hopes and dreams. I tried to step back and give people the time and space to tell their stories, to talk to one another, and pretty soon both the students and I began to feel that something special was happening.

Cecilia: It was kismet for me to work at the Open Book. I was finishing the WISH [Women In Self Help] program and Virginia, my teacher, told me to take the GED, I will pass it. I thought it's impossible, I was forty-six years old and I was not going to school since fourteen. So Virginia had given me the book and I studied in the house and I went and took the test one afternoon. Two weeks later I got the papers back that I passed the GED! I was very happy and I said I'm going to college but I heard about the job at the Open Book and I went for an interview. In the interview John says well, how do you feel about dealing with people who don't have an education? I said well I would like to help these people, you know; I'm not too old for that. I was just getting a divorce and before that I worked in a factory putting zippers on reversible skirts. I thought I had to do something and so I went to register for college. It was on a Friday. Saturday morning I got this call. This is John Gordon, I found out you passed the test, so you have no excuse not to take the job. He found out because he just spoke to his friend in the WISH program, so that is how I started working at the Open Book.

I remember when I began the classes we had this tiny place in the basement and in between these lockers they had these little, tiny chairs so it was uncomfortable but ... I remember talking to the students before I first started. I said you know that I have struggled too and I have struggled with reading and with studying. I know how difficult this is. I said you just ask me if you want any help. You know ... I can't give too much but I can give a little grain of sand; you know a few grains here, a few grains there, we make a beach. So that's what we're going to do here, we're going to start with a little grain of sand ...

Virginia: When I started I had just come to teach writing one day a week. At the time, I was getting divorced and my family was breaking up. Basically, I was looking for more hours because I already worked in another Good Shepherd program. The classes were extremely intimate; I loved the emphasis on people's lives ... even in the beginning when it was a really small program. We knew that it was people's lives that were important, including our own. Here, students were writing their own lives. I had never been in a place like this where students were in charge of the atmosphere.

Cecilia: Yes, I think that is a better way to learn for most of us, right? Like writing about the lives of the students. It was easy for them to read about what they wrote because it was better to read something you know about than something you don't know about. At the beginning I didn't have just one role. I would go and help John a little bit with the reading, an hour or so, but most of my job was answering the phone when he was in class. But then I started doing the counseling work. I watched John during the interviews and I thought I can do that. I liked doing the interviews.

Virginia: Cecilia, I always felt you really taught us a lot. You were a connection with what was real in terms of the students. Because the teachers were all from different backgrounds than the students, it was helpful to have someone who was in both worlds really.

Cecilia: I don't know why people thought I was so important because all I did was to love the students ... and I thought that what was between us was kind of an amazing thing ...

John: Do you remember that summer, I guess it was 1985, when the morning classes were finally able to move into our own space? At least it was our own space in the mornings. A bunch of students came in over that summer and together we painted the space and fixed up the classroom. We bought some tables and chairs so we didn't have to sit in those awful desks anymore. We wanted people to feel comfortable, to feel like adults. We wanted an atmosphere that was more like a group of friends sitting around a table in someone's kitchen. Even though it wasn't quite like that, we did set the tables up in the shape of a U so that people would be facing each other and they would be encouraged to talk to each other and not the teacher. The classroom was on the third floor with a lot of light. Florean, one of the students, started bringing in plants. She didn't ask; she just began doing it. She had grown up on a farm in the South and had a real way with plants. Soon the space was looking beautiful.

Virginia: Florean was such a classy, generous southern woman. She was about eighty years old with such a great history. She used to pick cotton when she was younger ... she could bake a sweet potato pie like you wouldn't believe. There were so many amazing students at the program. Ivan was also an incredible, thoughtful person and a very good writer. He helped a lot of other students tap into their own thoughts and put them into writing. He used to come very early and stay all afternoon, sometimes he even worked with the night students. He was from this neighborhood. He had a whole history of alcohol and drug abuse as a young man and it was too late for his liver really.... When he died, we named the library after him. The Open Book gave him this amazing tribute; we read his poetry and his family came. I remember this clearly because he had a lot of deaf members in his family and at the tribute they spoke with their hands, a whole crowd of people speaking to each other across the room by raising their hands.... I've never seen anything like it. At the Open Book, I always felt there was such a sense of safety and commitment—safety to be yourself and commitment that you weren't going to be thrown out. I mean even in liberal programs, students got put out just on the basis of attendance or because of personal problems.

Cecilia: I think somehow whoever came to the Open Book became part of a family. And I noticed that who didn't stay ...

Virginia: Didn't become a part of the family?

Cecilia: Yes. The ones that didn't get involved in the community, they left. The Open Book became not just a place but a group of people who were interested in participating in the life of the community in general. Even today I keep in touch with people who came to the Open Book and whose customs are so different, yet when they came to the Open Book they became part of the community.

John: It's interesting ... I mean students in other programs weren't such different people than at the Open Book, right? Who ends up there? Who ends up here? Why was it in one place you had certain issues and others you didn't? It's an interesting question. Why would one place be different?

*   *   *

From its very inception, it seemed the philosophy of the Open Book strove to model an alternative vision of society rooted in a more equitable, lovelier world that everyone at the program could co-create. The very first time I walked through the doors of the program, I too felt a powerful tug, an open invitation, almost a challenge, for people (students and instructors) to take as much control as possible over shaping the environment and culture of the program. For many, including myself, it was the first such invitation of its kind.

At the end of the preceding conversation, John raises an interesting question. If students aren't so very different in literacy programs across New York, then why would one place be so different? If the program existed in another place with other students, would it have been very different? Would it have attracted another set of extraordinary students? What set this program apart? John, Cecilia, and Virginia address some aspects of this issue in the preceding conversation:

• Space was created by both instructors and other students to talk about their lives, their struggles, their hopes and dreams. Students' words and dreams were woven into various levels of the program. This was one of the many ways the Open Book attempted to place students at the center.

• Almost from the very beginning, the idea that people were more than just classmates to each other began to emerge. Ivan staying after school and working with students on their writing helped to establish peer-teaching as an important aspect of the school. It also signaled to other students that this place was not one that they needed to leave when class was over. By feeling welcomed to stay afterward, they were playing a part in shaping the culture of this being truly their school. When Cecilia relates her own struggles, she sets up a dynamic that teachers weren't the only experts in the room. Co-teaching and co-learning happened simultaneously among students and instructors. By pointing to the ways her own experiences mirrored students', she lets students know that she's an insider to important aspects of their lived realities. She has walked in their shoes of lived experiences and shared their culture in authentic ways that others who hadn't shared those sets of experiences never could. She lets them know that a world of shared understanding lies between them. As Cunningham (2000) states, the concept of co-learners flattens the hierarchical structure. This doesn't mean that the instructor has very different information than the learner; what it does assume is that the position of knowledge producer and knowledge consumer can be regularly transposed between them through participation in praxis (p. 584).

• The knowledge students brought to the program was honored, taken seriously. Cecilia refers to people becoming a family over time, to the program being a space where it was possible for people who were interested in participating in the life of the community to do so. People were made to feel more than just a statistic. As Ornelas (1997) says, a person cannot plan to teach another person but they can live a process together (p. 145).

• The power of the collective emerges from people's words. People's joined efforts, knowledge, voices, or strength unquestionably far surpass any one individual's and there is undeniable power in numbers (Heaney, personal conversation, December 2006).

• Entire bodies of research support students' writing about their lives, honoring the important, powerful things they have to say when space is made to listen as those stories emerge. Engagement theories point out that when learning begins where people are, they learn faster. By inviting students to bring their culture into the classroom, shared meanings and identities can be fostered. This type of learning stimulates student participation and enhances students' capacity to remember what was learned by making connections to their lives (Auerbach, 1992; Curtis, 1990; Purcell-Gates, 2000).

• Cecilia's comments point to the emphasis the Open Book staff put on listening to people and acknowledging all that they brought to the program—by supporting them in not feeling "lesser than," where they were treated with dignity and not dehumanized—which opened up many options for exciting possibilities both in and out of the classroom. An example of this would be Cecilia's role in the program, which grew over time from secretary to counselor. From seemingly small gestures such as students sitting facing each other to larger ones such as students voluntarily staying to work with other students after class, it became exceedingly clear that to many people there the program was much more than just a school. Time and time again former students talked about the way they became a family to each other. There was a sense of love and community running like an invisible river, gentle waves lapping their way through the corridors, causing thousands of unseen ripples that ran deep into the core of the program.

• Many students at the Open Book (as in other literacy programs) were poor or working-class people of color. In our society, poor people are marginalized and ignored in myriad ways and the only real power they might have to effect change is collectively, through their numbers (Freire, 1970; Heaney, 2000). It was my strong sense that at the Open Book, there was recognition of this and a vision that perhaps, if participants' voices were listened to in developing the culture of the program, it would then be a viable possibility for those participants to go out to their communities and be agents of change. One of the central tenets was that ordinary people (as defined by the dominant culture) were valuable and collectively had the power to not only change their community but reshape society.

What were some other, more intangible, yet potent characteristics of the program that continued to set it apart from more mainstream literacy programs? Was it the way it defined its role in working with students? Was it the way it perceived the purpose of education? Or was it a combination of something else altogether? In the upcoming chapter, three students from the Open Book reflect on some of these qualities that set the Open Book apart from the majority of programs in the NYC adult literacy world.

📖

TWO

Education Not by the Book!

Three Students' Journeys

In this chapter three students (Edami, Antonia, and Hazel) talk about their individual journeys to and through the Open Book and share some of the reasons the program was so important to them. Edami was a student at the Open Book from 1991 to 1996. She originally lived in the community (South Brooklyn) but was one of many forced out with the gentrification of the area. Both her mother and brother also attended the program. Though never a member of committees in the program, she often stayed after class and worked with other students, connecting with many of her classmates in informal ways, and through that process, emerged as one of the leaders in the program. She also was a prolific writer, and many other students in the program came to know her through her writing. Her stories, gripping and raw, explored the theme of abuse in her life. They were published by the program and had a tremendous impact on many students.

Antonia and Hazel were students in the program from 1997 to 2000 and were classmates in Virginia's class. Several people had mentioned Antonia's and Hazel's thoughtfulness so I knew their voices would be valuable additions to the already rich and flavorful gumbo of perspectives I had been engaged in dialogue with. However, Hazel was challenging to contact. Everyone I spoke with seemed to have lost contact with her. However, one person did have an old address so I wrote her a letter. In my brief note to her, I explained that I was attempting to document this program's history, and while hopeful for a response, I acknowledged that my chances were fairly slim. However, one Sunday evening, a week after posting the note, my telephone at home rang. The voice on the other end announced it belonged to Hazel. The second announcement she made was that the only reason she was responding to my note was that this was regarding the Open Book and that her experience there had been a profound one. She followed that by unequivocally stating that were I from any other adult literacy program she had attended, she would not have availed herself to speak with me.

In the following conversation, Antonia, Hazel, and Edami share some of their thoughts with Virginia on why they felt the program was unique.

*　*　*

Antonia: I had been in and out of programs for a long time. I would end up leaving programs because they weren't giving me what I was looking for. One day I decided to go to the library and get a listing of all the GED programs that were available. I knew I needed to find a program close to home because I needed to pick the kids up from school. Every day I looked at the list but I just never noticed the Open Book. I found another program on the list and was about to register but something told me to go back and look at the sheet again. That was when I found the Open Book! So the next day, after I dropped my son off to art class, I walked to Twelfth Street. I'm a spiritual person so for me it was a sign to find the Open Book on that piece of paper.

Hazel: I had been trying other places but they would always ask me to write an essay before I could be accepted and I could never do it. I remember I was so scared when I first went to the Open Book. I think that was why I came off so strong. I was on the defense, trying to protect myself. You know after trying and trying different programs, you get broken down. Your self-esteem goes way down.

Edami: I went to other programs but I didn't even stay to register. I don't know why but I didn't feel like I belonged there. I would even make the registration appointments but once I showed up I knew I couldn't go through with it. I would just run down the stairs and leave. I knew they were places I couldn't stay. But from the moment I went upstairs to the Open Book I saw people sitting at tables working in groups. It felt so free. I remember one group talking about everything they were going to do. I observed them talking and was so moved. After joining the program I became one of them. You couldn't shut me up!

Antonia: That's true. They always made me think that there wasn't anyone who couldn't do it. There was always a feeling of togetherness, I felt like we all got strength from each other.

Hazel: I still have that feeling inside me that I can do anything. I really do feel like if I didn't go to the Open Book, I wouldn't have gotten my GED. I wouldn't have attempted to go back to school or do anything more with my life. After the Open Book I attended Kingsborough Community College [one of the campuses for the City University of New York] and I now have a certificate so I can open my own daycare. But even though I know I'm moving forward I still feel sometimes like I'm holding back. This feeling of doubt, it's in my soul, my being, it's saying if I could spell, I could do anything ... it keeps me back. My mother was never a philosopher of staying in school so I couldn't really go to her for anything. I went through my whole schooling without any support.

Antonia: I know that if I hadn't bumped into the Open Book, I wouldn't have my GED today either. It was the only place that told me I could do it, that dared me to try.

Edami: The Open Book changed my whole life. I felt like I opened a door and found everything I was looking for on the other side. It made me feel like a person, like I was somebody; that I could do whatever I want. Now, people see me as someone who's smart and open. Before the Open Book I used to go to psychiatrists. I never told them an inch of my stories. Nothing! I didn't even know who I was. I knew my name was Edami but who was Edami? What did she want from life? By the time I left the Open Book, I knew who I was, and what I went through. I knew I wanted to be a supervisor; I ended up becoming a supervisor. My sister passed away and I promised her I would run the marathon; I did that. I knew I wanted to ride in the bike-a-thon; I did that too. I feel like I was able to do all those things because I participated in the Open Book. I used to be so closed before, so afraid, my self-esteem was beyond low but somehow in the Open Book, I just let it all out. It was a place I could go and learn to trust, to let myself be me. We protected each other's words and values. I felt free to say and do what I wanted. There was a sense of safety and trust in the program and I knew that nobody could hurt me again. I knew that we would protect each other's words and I've taken those feelings with me.

Virginia: Edami, I remember people were especially affected by your stories. They were talking about them for years, especially "Bearing Pain" and "The Broken Black Dress." People could just feel what you were saying and they remembered it forever.

Edami: In my life I had to deal with a lot of abuse. I wrote this piece when we were writing our autobiographies for a book of student writing. It was about when my husband and I went to a party and a guy asked me to dance. I told him no but I saw my husband give me one of his looks that could kill. I tried to pretend nothing happened but he pulled me by my hair into the street. On our way out, he slapped me. I was crying but he wouldn't stop. As we were crossing the street, there was a car coming our way. He pushed me toward the car and grabbed the back of my dress and ripped it a little. I started to scream because I thought he was going to kill me. When we got home, forget it. He went crazy on me. He ripped my dress into pieces. I just sat on the bed looking at my beautiful, black dress broken into little pieces of shreds. The next day I left him, but he found me and like a fool I went back. I still think the worst experience was the rug. Every time I see a rug, I see myself wrapped up in it. I overcame a lot of that through writing. That was my best therapy, just writing everything down.

Hazel: I remember writing an essay about that entire struggle I went through when I left home in Trinidad and came to the United States. Virginia was the only person that showed interest and who ever asked me to talk about this. For me that essay was the breaking point. I needed somebody to read it who would care, who wouldn't judge me.

Antonia: When we read other students' books, we were learning who these people were and somehow the stories gave me the freedom not to worry about spelling. Writing at the Open Book was about feelings, expressions. It was a little like art. Some people paint to express themselves. We actually were able to enjoy expressing ourselves through writing. But it meant Virginia had a lot of correcting to do.

Virginia: Not corrections, just possibly revealing the words. We treated students' books as serious literature because they were. You were all so amazing that you were writing the curriculum. We read your writing with other classes many times after you left.

Antonia: I think that's why the Open Book was so special. They focused on our needs and how to fill those through education. Not just education by the book. We discussed slavery, unions, and the importance of voting. Most of us there didn't think our voice mattered; we thought we didn't matter. I learned to let things in. I remember I had this friend who graduated from college and whenever she would invite my husband and me to go to dinner, I would always make an excuse not to go because I was afraid of sitting and eating with someone who went to college. But at the Open Book I learned we were equal and that the teachers could learn from us.

Hazel: I remember my son coming to me one day. Mommy, help me with my spelling. I said, I can't help you with your spelling unless you give me that sheet. I had to explain to my ten-year-old that his mommy couldn't read above his level. But when I went to the Open Book, I didn't have a disability there.

Antonia: We were each other's heroes there.

Virginia: It was just so unusual for teachers at a program to see their job as working with a person's soul, their essential self, to start from people's strengths rather than see students as something that needed to be fed knowledge. You know the experience of it still feeds me up to this day.

Edami: It's like you take it with you, it's something you can't forget.

Hazel: I think programs need to understand that they need to have people who could understand what the students are going through, who can relate to students rather than the mechanical system of the government. They need to understand that you can't teach somebody unless that person is comfortable in the program.

Antonia: Although we are adults, we come to these programs because something in our lives didn't go right. Something didn't happen in school for us and we need encouragement. We need to hear, You can do this. We need to hear that it doesn't matter what level you are, you can bring yourself higher. Most of us at the Open Book would say they didn't have someone who cared and encouraged them. We need someone to say you're not just another number passing through here, you're a human being and you came here with so many struggles and dreams. Teachers could make the world of difference if they just saw their students as human beings, gave them some encouragement, and treated them with dignity and respect. They need to understand that most of these people are poor, people who have struggled. I think I was one of the more fortunate ones to come through the program. I am married, I have a good relationship with my husband, and I have my children. In a lot of ways I wasn't struggling. But I came to the program as a person prepared to fail again and I think that teachers in programs need to be open to that. They need to ask, What can I do for you? Is there anyone here who didn't get it? Do you understand what's happening?

Hazel: I think the main thing about the Open Book was that they never really followed the book. We took care of each other and brought each other up. We never left anybody behind. I always thought I was at the bottom of the barrel. But by the time I left the Open Book, I knew I could climb out.

Antonia: The Open Book tried to change the system, not follow it. It was successful because the teachers followed their hearts, not rules. I remember a few years ago, John took me to a meeting where all the directors would gather to discuss the program. I sat there listening to all these people making these decisions about how the program should run and I felt most of them didn't have a clue what students really needed.

* * *

In the preceding section, all three students speak of attending multiple adult literacy programs but not finding what they were looking for. Edami says she just felt as if she didn't really belong in other programs but almost magically, guided by a deep intuitive sense, from almost the first moment upon entering the Open Book, felt enveloped by a spirit of community that seemed to reach out and beckon. How exactly could this culture be planted and nurtured in other programs? Whose seeds would be planted by whom? Both Antonia and Edami mention feeling instinctively and inexplicably that this place felt "right" to them, and continue to emphatically attribute current successes and accomplishments in their lives to this program.

• Even though Hazel has unquestionably accomplished so much (obtained her GED and a daycare license while raising her children, etc.) she still retains this nagging sense of self-doubt deep in her soul, whispering to her all the things she isn't or can't do, this tiny voice that she says ends up holding her back from accomplishing even more. The scars inflicted on her by the school system seem to continue to affect her ability to transcend and transform the identity imposed on her by the dominant culture. Despite tangible accomplishments, she continues to perceive herself as having a deficiency. Do these scars ever get ejected from our consciousness? Will they ever from mine? Do we ever realize that maybe, just maybe, the deficiency could lie with the way school is structured and not with us? According to Kucer (2001), because the beliefs of dominant groups so permeate the society we live in and because individuals so seldom encounter alternative perspectives, they may come to view these beliefs not as socially constructed, but as normative, universal. Nesbit (2004) echoes this by pointing out that if we believe this reality is universal, then we don't question that schools and other educational institutions serve as places to foster characteristics of passivity, conformity, productivity, and competition. We don't deconstruct this socially constructed reality: that by promoting these beliefs of passivity, competition, and productivity as superior, the larger social mechanisms of capitalism go unexamined and remain intact. Whose interest does this benefit? (p. 19).

• As Stuckey (1991) states, we have seen that access to a literate economy is through education. We have seen that the arbiter of education is the test. We have seen that the test reduces to poverty or maintains in it entire segments of our economy (p. 118). What we have to see, also, is how literacy is a weapon, the knife that severs the society and slices the opportunities and rights of its poorest people. Thus, the questions of literacy are questions of oppression; they are matters of enforcement, maintenance, acquiescence, internalization, revolution. Stuckey (1991) adds, when societies dissolve the forms of oppression against their own citizens and against other societies, then they will dissolve the questions of literacy also. Only when the forms of oppression are undermined can the question of what to do with one's life become central (p. 64).

• Edami seems able to name her own transformation and journey through the program. She describes both how she perceives herself and how others perceive her as being radically altered. She seems able to access entirely new words and worlds and attributes this to her journey through this program. She talks about feeling safe, learning to trust, and feeling a sense of protection from being part of the group, that the group will protect her from harm and nothing can ever hurt her again. In those words lie such faith and belief in being part of a group and also the other members of that group. What would programs need to have in place to foster similar statements and feelings from students? Virginia undoubtedly played a role in the development of this culture of trust that had taken root in the class, but students also undeniably contributed in critical ways to this invisible yet precious quality that had blossomed within the program; they played an essential role in mixing the magical potion that acted as a healing salve on old wounds and a protectant against new ones forming. The three women's words involved the group sharing, reflecting, and encouraging each other through difficult personal issues. Freire (1985) states, to study is not to consume ideas but to create and re-create them (p. 4).

• From Edami's story we're able to glimpse some of the trauma and hurt inflicted on students by their partners, the school system, poverty, and other markers of the dehumanizing culture we live in (Macedo, 1994). Many students came to the program with similar stories of incredibly difficult issues that they were struggling with in their personal lives and often with no real support network in place, from homelessness to domestic abuse to battling and negotiating hostile systems daily in order to survive. Though Edami's story may initially read as laced with elements of sensationalism, it reflects her reality and the reality of many adult literacy students. At the Open Book, there was a commitment to work with students on the bigger issues, a recognition that students came to the program with difficult lives and that space was made to acknowledge this. Yet there is something else going on as well. Edami, Antonia, and Hazel all exhibit remarkable resilience of spirit, deep strength, and an ability to heal and to continue to hope. It almost seemed as if the Open Book represented a sanctuary for our collective souls against further onslaught from the dominant world, a chance for us to heal ourselves and support each other to do the same. A chance to remake ourselves in entirely new, whole ways, to become actors and rewrite the script imposed on us. Some of the pain inflicted by society is reflected in Antonia's experience of not being able to spend time with someone who had attended college, somehow considering herself to not be worthy enough. It's as if as members living in this society, we somehow begin to see ourselves as things that can be bought and sold, a package of personality assets with a value attached, but not one in which we had any part in determining or defining. Someone who attends college has a higher value placed on them. Where does this message originate that our personal qualities and traits can be bartered like goods at market value as part of an exchange economy? Yet, miraculously it seems as if all three of the women are able to partially cast off the thick, scaly identities (if only temporarily) they've lived with for years and that society constructed for them to wear at least long enough to glimpse another less scarred self underneath. Hazel says she didn't have a disability at the Open Book. Antonia says she realized teachers could learn from them. Who decides whether you have a disability or not? Who are the children in disability classes? What color? At what cost? Do so few spaces exist in our society where people are treated with respect and dignity? Where they aren't further marginalized or oppressed? Is the magic spell we created together at the Open Book so potent that this experience will forever reside in our hearts and nourish our souls, sustaining us through further indignities inflicted by the dominant system?

• Edami, Hazel, and Antonia all speak about self-esteem. Antonia talks about being afraid to sit and eat with someone who had attended college. Hazel talks about her self-esteem being broken down over time, and Edami says her self-esteem was beyond low. I've been thinking a lot recently about the word *self-esteem*, its implications, and how it's used. I have seen the socially constructed ways in which this word is used. There is an underlying assumption that our image of ourselves can somehow be separated or disconnected from the one society has imposed on us without any recognition of one's relationship to the larger society and the many ways in which our selves are merged with and are reflections of society's perceptions of us. Moreover, isn't this term inextricably bound to concepts of race and class? To what extent does self-esteem promote a concept of individualism in mainstream culture that says we can somehow improve our bad feelings about ourselves without any connection to the oppressive economic structure we live in? This economic structure dictates to and bombards poor people of color with messages that make them ashamed or embarrassed about who they are. (It says, "Buy this item; it will change your life." But what if I can't afford to buy it?) How possible is it to discuss notions of self-esteem without unearthing larger issues of inequity centered on poverty, race, and individualism in society? Is it possible not to internalize others' perceptions of us?

• All three women appeal to staff and administrators in other literacy programs to treat students with respect, and with love instead of as a quantitative requirement to maintain funding. What would that respect and love look like and how would they manifest themselves on an everyday basis? Between teachers and students? Between students and students? Between teachers and teachers? How could instructors and students facilitate this journey in programs so that students don't race down the stairs like Edami before even registering? How could literacy workers be supported in adopting this shift? How could changes in a more humanizing direction be sustained in community literacy programs and in the discussions that shape policy? How could this shift occur without the systems that currently promote structural inequities also shifting? As Allman (1999) states, simply verbally denouncing social injustice while leaving intact the structures of society that promote this inequity and poverty is ineffective.

• Finally, Antonia and Hazel speak of the Open Book attempting to change the system and the status quo. Sissel (1996) points out that as adult educators, we cannot do more of the same anymore. It hasn't worked and won't work (Sissel, 1996). Students and administrators must look at the options that exist and ask about the purpose of literacy education in America today. Who has defined this purpose? Students? Teachers? Or as Antonia wonders, are they people who have no idea what students really need? As Sheared (personal communication, 2006) states, we must find ways to ensure questions are being asked and honest conversation is happening with people who could effect action. Scipio Colin III (personal communication, 2005) points out that there are thousands of bodies floating down a river. Literacy workers within the current system manage to pull out one or two or even several, but is anyone attending to the source of the river, questioning why these bodies are falling in? Is anyone doing the work and guarding the river to make sure they don't keep falling or getting thrown in? It's clear the source of the river has been left unattended for some time. The question for the field is, What is our mandate?

And what about the students who weren't interested in a program that emphasized collectivity and who weren't interested in a program that fostered a more democratic society? What about students who didn't see adult literacy as being rooted in larger social inequities? Who instead wanted a more authoritarian style that reflected their earlier school experiences (which were most likely unsuccessful as related through the many painful stories students shared regarding their prior school histories) and that didn't serve their best interests? Were we being fair to them? Had we appointed ourselves as heat-seeking missiles of oppression (Brookfield, 2005)?

Three

An Invitation Inside Our Classrooms

A Different Way of Teaching Reading and Writing

What about students for whom education signified worksheets, drills, and other traditional activities? Who request their current education to reflect principles familiar to their prior educational experiences? What about when they expect the instructor to do most of the talking and not ask for any of their input? If we, as literacy workers, claim to build a program around what students say they want, then shouldn't we respect students' requests? According to Auerbach (1992) it's very difficult for anyone to ask for something they've never experienced, something they may have no idea actually exists, or even could exist. In some ways, it can be compared to looking at the items offered on a menu and then ordering a totally different dish, one that you think would be much more flavorful and dynamic. Most of us order from the options presented to us. Not only is it difficult to concoct an alternative dish in our heads, but even if we do, we may not think our request will be met with a very positive reaction or we may think we have no right to ask for anything other than the list of presented options.

Very often the menu of learning options that has been placed in front of us most of our lives has been a teacher-directed approach, and even though it almost certainly didn't work in students' best interests, in my experience there's often an internalized perception that tests and worksheets, chalk and talk, drill and de-skill all legitimize what education should look like. The main model most students (including myself) have been exposed to was top-down, where the teacher most likely didn't involve students in decision-making, where the instructor controlled most of what happened in class. The teacher was perceived as being the only expert in the room, the only

19

knowledgeable one. Yet, if this model is successful, why do adult literacy programs exist? Why is there the need for so many more? Isn't it because the school system failed so many students that there is such a strong and urgent need for adult literacy programs?

Giroux (2001, p. 225) makes us aware that literacy can be neither neutral nor objective, and that for the most part it is inscribed in the ideology and practice of domination. Freire (1970, p. 74) adds that the oppressed have always been inside the structure that has made them beings for others. The solution is not to integrate them into the structure of oppression but to transform the structure so that they can become beings for themselves.

My colleagues and I at the Open Book believed it was important to have ongoing conversations with students around this issue because we knew that many students would probably find new and unfamiliar ways of approaching teaching and learning to be initially daunting. At the Open Book there was a sense that if issues were put on the table in honest and transparent ways and negotiated, if an invitation instead of a mandate was put forth, then new spaces and possibilities of teaching and learning would open up.

What then is the significance of building a program around themes and issues reflective of students' lives? Of asking students at the beginning of class what they are interested in studying and using what they say as the basis of units of study for further analysis and action? Of taking into account the issues their communities were grappling with, their culture and family backgrounds, and considering all of these gifts to be honored, sources of strength instead of something broken in need of fixing or something to be trampled on? In many ways, it is about disrupting and subverting the status quo. To many students who walked into the Open Book, school represented pain and disappointment, a place lacking in hope and meaning. One student was told by his teacher in seventh grade, "You should concentrate on building up your body because it's too late for your mind," and "Don't bother speaking until you have something to say that is worth listening to." Another student said, "I don't even know what my teacher's face looked like, all he did was write on the blackboard and we were supposed to take notes. It was too hard for me so I just left. I was sure it was going to be the same setup at the Open Book where I was put in a corner with a book and told this is what you need to do. This was my last try; if I didn't make it here, that was it. I wasn't going to make it ever!" I heard what seemed like countless stories similar in pain, reflective of the thoughtlessness or neglect inflicted by the school system, that resulted in deep, bleeding gashes to many students' consciousness and hearts. For students who never see stories of their own culture reflected in the pages of any book they read, imperceptibly a sense of not being good enough quietly envelops them, settles over their shoulders, becomes a heavy cloak weighing heavily on them. The instructors were determined that this wouldn't be the case at the Open Book.

There were ongoing conversations discussing the deliberate (though some may argue well intentioned) and repeated assault, the ways through which mainstream culture was privileging the words of one segment of the population over the others. At the Open Book, instructors, along with students, attempted to examine the ways in which the words of the wealthy and powerful were privileged over those belonging to ordinary people. People at the Open Book made the conscious decision not to reproduce the culture of schooling in this program. If so many students failed under that system, we knew there was something deeply flawed with the system, or rather the system (through well-intentioned people who were complicit and may have inadvertently upheld the culture) was perpetuating the status quo and keeping power in the hands of a select few while large segments of society continued to be oppressed and poor. It was therefore important to confront and be conscious of the societal structures that had promoted their economic marginalization. As Stuckey (1991, p. 64) points out, educational systems oppress, and it is less important whether the oppression is systematic and intentional, though often it is both, than that it works against freedom.

Heath (1983), in a groundbreaking study, found that schools favored and promoted middle-class values. In her study exploring how three different groups of people used literacy to negotiate their worlds, she discovered that school is a direct extension of middle-class literacy patterns. Children who don't follow middle-class literacy patterns (which schools privilege) are at an instant disadvantage that only increases over time. When educators fail to acknowledge or honor the strengths of students from homes that are not middle class, another door of opportunity and access will be shut firmly on them. Testing is an important part of middle-class culture because traditional literacy education begins in ideas of the dominant or mainstream culture. Education becomes about a need to conform. Would the middle-class culture conform to nondominant ways of knowing? Not likely. In our society today, being a member of the dominant culture provides access to opportunities and social currency. The teaching of literacy, an extension of this culture, then becomes a regulation of access, politics, and power (Stuckey, 1991).

In classes, teachers and students attempted to analyze and make transparent how these systems worked and who benefited most from them staying intact. We, the instructors along with the students in the program, imagined what it might be like if we lived in a society where wealth was more evenly distributed among all of its members. If we believed that learning began and ended with the students, then it made sense for the curriculum to be planned and negotiated with students, to contain their stories and struggles. In that vein, the instructors would talk with students about what they wanted to study that year. In the following conversation, one such example is chronicled through the class writing a play together about the housing crisis affecting many students. This story, which took place within the first two years of the program, was then published in one of the student journals for students in other classes at the Open Book as well as other literacy programs around NYC to read and discuss.

*   *   *

A Glimpse into the Production of *Welcome Back, Lucy*

John: We tried to build the curriculum around the ideas and concerns that the students were raising in the classroom. This meant that the teachers had to be paying a lot of attention to what the students were talking about, what they wanted. It's definitely a lot more work for the teachers, but in the end a lot more exciting. Those first two years, I remember the neighborhood where we were located was changing very fast. Landlords were letting buildings run down, trying to force tenants out. And when apartments became empty, the landlords would fix them up and charge very high rents or sell them as co-ops. And I remember it seemed like every day one student or another would come in with a story of what was happening in their building—another awful tale about their landlords. A number of students were in and out of housing court. Some were living in buildings that had been abandoned by the landlords. Still others were on the edge of homelessness.

So we started studying about the housing crisis. I brought in some readings that tried to explain why all these changes were occurring and some readings on tenants' rights. I asked students to write about their apartments and their feelings on what was happening with housing in the city. We started debating what should be done. I used to copy down what people said, take the notes home, type them up, and bring them back the next day. We would read it together and debate some more. One day Maria said, "John, why don't we do a play? We know a lot about this." Now, I knew something about housing but nothing about putting on plays, so the idea made me nervous. But I screwed up my courage and said, "That sounds like a great idea! What do people think?" Most of the students liked the idea but some didn't.

We decided to go ahead with the idea, and for the next month or two spent a lot of time in class working on the play. Students would take parts, and we would sit around, making up lines. One day everyone became a landlord and we acted out a landlords' lunch. Another day we did a visit to the landlord's office by the tenants.

I remember one rehearsal very clearly. It involved two students, Cathy and Yolande. Cathy was playing Lucy, the central character in the play. She was a very timid woman, on welfare. Her landlord wanted to throw her out and was harassing her as much as possible. Yolande was playing Mary, a tough woman, an immigrant who wouldn't let anyone put her down. Lucy says she's afraid of her landlord; there's nothing she can do.

Yolande says, "What do you mean? You have rights. You have to stick up for yourself. This is a free country."

Cathy all of a sudden was on fire. "You don't understand! When you are on welfare, you have no rights. They make you do this, they make you do that, they can take away your money like that."

Before our eyes, Cathy and Yolande had stopped acting. The debate they were having was real, and for those few minutes, they became their characters. It was a powerful moment. I believe they each realized some things about the other and themselves. In the end, we wrote a play and performed it for a small audience. We called it, "Welcome Back, Lucy." (To read the entire play, please go to Appendix B.) There were great moments, although many of them were in rehearsals. The process of the play was very exciting but a little difficult. Some of the students didn't want to participate. One student complained that it was boring. Some of the other students who were playing important roles started getting cold feet. They'd be absent from school on the days we were planning to rehearse. On top of everything else, Florean, who was to play an important role, took a cab to school that day instead of her usual bus and the cab got into an accident. She wound up in the hospital instead of our play. Another student had to sit in for her at the last moment.

An Excerpt from *Welcome Back, Lucy!*

Conclusion: Lucy Comes Back to Visit

Ms. Smith: How are you making it, girl?

Lucy: Not very good. I listened to the landlord. He said he'd get me another apartment, but now I'm at the shelter.

Mrs. Brown: We told you we'd help you. Why didn't you come to us?

Lucy: I didn't listen. I was afraid. I should have stayed here. I should have listened to what you said. I should have listened to what May said. Now they want to take my kids away.

   The first two days I was in the park. I'm begging people on the streets for a quarter. You have to sleep with one eye open, one eye closed. Sometimes you sleep on a roof, sometimes underneath a trailer. Now you're out on the street, you don't know what you're doing. You're out there picking up stuff from the street every night, sleeping under trailers. You don't know when someone might rape you. A cop saw me crying. The children were hungry. The cop took me to the shelter. It's not real nice, but at least the kids have something to eat. Everyone sleeps in one big room. All the cots are together, there's no privacy. You have to watch your kids. Sometimes men use the women's bathrooms.

(All of a sudden there's a knock on the door.)

Mrs. Brown: Come in.

(The door opens, and all the other tenants walk in.)

Everybody: Hey, Lucy! Lucy, how you doing? Welcome back, Lucy!

(Everybody comes together around Lucy and hugs her. Then they all join hands on the table.)

Narrator: This is happening to thousands of people: the poor and the middle class are being driven out of their homes; children are being taken out of schools. It's happening to a lot of people, and we should keep fighting.

The End

*   *   *

Writing played a central role at the Open Book. Stacie (an evening instructor in the program from 1990 to 1994), John, and Virginia reflect on how seriously people's writing was treated. Students read one another's writing with the same respect one would a more "famous" writer. They got to know each other and then became friends through reading each other's writing. Gradually students came to regard themselves as "real" writers. Writing was something they did for pleasure, to discover meaning; it was not just an unfulfilling exercise one had to go through in order to pass the GED exam.

Stacie: I think the Open Book really did a good job of helping not only teachers but also students see the importance of publishing student writing. I've been to other programs where student writing has been published but not as much and not as seriously with actual nice-looking books. I think that's something I've tried to bring into other places where I've worked and I think it was really made very clear how important that was when I was at the Open Book.

John: Do you remember we had actually gotten a grant from the State that year associated with student leadership? At the end of that year we wrote a history of the Open Book called "We're All in This Together" (though I didn't necessarily think we were all in this together but one of the students came up with that title), which was mostly anecdotal. A group of us met over the summer and we ended up mixing the history of the school with our conversations around writing the book. We married the section that you wrote, Stacie, to what we wrote.

Virginia: I just thought writing was a really important part of the atmosphere of the Open Book. People's writing was considered serious literature. I remember Edami's [a student at the Open Book who shares her story in Chapter 2] stories really affecting so many people, people outside the Open Book.

*   *   *

The topic of the play offers a concrete example of how an issue affecting students' lives could be the basis for deeper analysis while at the same time addressing reading and writing proficiency. Adult learning theory and other research tell us that students tend to be more engaged if the unit of study emerges from real concerns in their lives (Auerbach, 1992; Shor, 1987).

• The process of writing a play together reflects a spirit of engagement (though as mentioned, not everyone managed to maintain enthusiasm all the time and not everyone chose to write a play; but the idea itself was born from a student's suggestion). By connecting the world inside the classroom to the larger societal context of the outside world, opportunities for learning and making meaning expand. Students could use the classroom to discover and discuss perspectives they had about their worlds. Research (Martin, 2001; Purcell-Gates and Waterman, 2000) recognizes it is impossible to separate sociopolitical issues when working with adult literacy students, and recommends that practitioners focus on themes central to students' oppression or marginalization. To do less is to continue to marginalize students by wasting their time with superficial topics that affirm the status quo and trivialize the education process (Purcell-Gates and Waterman, 2000, p. 115). Freire (1970) adds that an education program that fails to respect the particular view of the world held by the people being educated constitutes cultural invasion, good intentions notwithstanding. The Open Book's students and staff made a sincere effort not to replicate the culture of schooling within this program. This attempt didn't always work; there were students who wanted prepackaged activities, and not every student wanted to be a part of creating a community. While it might have been less interesting, it certainly would have been easier to sit and fulfill someone else's commands instead of being asked to think about what this classroom could look like. Did each student in the program play an equal role in making decisions? No, but there was a committed effort to create space to be involved and to many students like Maria, it was a chance to rewrite the label imposed and stamped on her identity by society; it was an opportunity to reject it.

• Inherent in this unit of study about the housing crisis is the acknowledgment that education can never be neutral. Everything we as practitioners do or don't do, say or leave unsaid in the classroom, reflects a political stance, whether we ourselves recognize it or not. As Horton (1998) said, there is no such thing as neutrality. Instead, he says neutrality is synonymous for aligning with the existing system, following the crowd, being what the system wants you to be.

• When students write a play together, they share an opportunity to become authors of knowledge they have co-constructed instead of consumers of someone else's concepts (Hull, 1997). Through this experience, opportunities emerge for students transforming their worlds through words. Writing becomes an act of making space for voices to be heard, voices that have been suppressed or ignored. Rich (1994) says, if the imagination is to transcend and transform experience, it has to question, to challenge, to conceive of alternatives, perhaps to the very life you live at this moment. "You have to be free to play around with notions that day might be night, love might be hate, and nothing can be too sacred for the imagination to call experience by another name. For writing is renaming" (p. 43). At the Open Book writing was a central aspect of the culture of the program. As Virginia says in Chapter 1, students were writing their own lives.

• Research points to the Language Experience Approach (LEA) as a valuable strategy to teach reading (Goodman, 1996). First, by writing down exactly what students say and using those words as text, students learn to read their own words. There's already a level of familiarity and level of engagement between the student and those words. Second, by using the exact words of students as text, there's a certain legitimizing of not only what the student says but how she says it.

• It is important for writing to be meaningfully linked to students' contexts and lives, for space and opportunity to be present for them to locate their own voice and author their own stories. There is value when students write for authentic purposes and audiences, not a decontextualized drill from a generic workbook requesting they write about their favorite holiday. (Though there is nothing inherently problematic about a holiday activity, when the class is solely built on those and similar learning tasks, the spaces to remake what learning could look like are diminished.)

• When opportunities for real education occurs, the kind of education where students are respected as serious writers and serious thinkers, options are opened up in how they perceive themselves and how they're perceived by others, worlds are transformed, and shackles unchained. What happens among students in that classroom becomes magical; the classroom emerges as a space of limitless possibilities waiting to be discovered. As Freire (1970) points out, without dialogue there is no real communication, and without communication there can be no true education.

Over time this model of instruction blossomed and grew. Soon many exciting things were being attempted and studied in different classes. Not all of them were successes but there was a feeling that the Open Book community learned what worked most successfully in teaching and learning by being open to trying different, new ways of seeing, thinking, and doing. Another example of this type of instruction was from Stephanie Lawson, an instructor who taught at the program from 1986 to 1990 and who (together with her students) called people's attention to the power and value of people's stories, someone who moved the program in the direction of community storytelling. In summing up examples of experiences reflective of her teaching, she recalls:

Stephanie: After reading an oral history project done by a class at
another community-based organization in the Bronx, we decided
to do our own. I taped students' testimonies about their lives and
learning experiences. With hardly any prompting students would
talk and talk. I typed them up and we read them in class. We went
through each story together. I then applied for a small grant to print
these in booklet form, which we were able to get. It was great, a
morale lifter and something to share in the wider adult education
community.

We also did a soap opera called "The Class Story," after reading
"Sudz," a soap opera written by another class. We did one chapter
per class, for an hour once a week, of a story of people in Brooklyn. I
gave students the first sentence, "Tony walked down Third Avenue,"
and they took off from there. It made great reading material with
adult themes. Some testimonies of hardship and abuse were painful
to read at times, and I see this happening at all as a result of that
atmosphere of respect and honoring the sharing of knowledge. We
saw how people prevailed. Learning in the program included strong
emotions and was more integrative in our lives.

The booklet Stephanie refers to became *Four Stories: Oral Histories from
the Open Book.* (To read one of the life histories from *Four Stories,* see Appendix C.) The four students whose stories, told in their own voices, make
up the sixty-eight-page booklet were listed on the front cover as authors.
Five hundred copies were kept at the program and the other half were distributed to other adult education programs. This booklet offers a concrete
example of how extraordinary ordinary people's words and lives were. It
respected and cherished their courage and determination as well as documented their struggles around poverty and lack of education. This text
was read, discussed, critiqued, analyzed, and remembered by students
in other classes at the program as well as other literacy programs. It was
an important step in establishing a serious culture of writing within the
program and invited a collective dialogue among students and instructors in different adult literacy programs in NYC to discuss different roles
writing could play in the cultural development of their programs. Like
two invisible but welcome guests, safety and trust sat among the students
throughout this process and without them present in this process of deep
sharing, this book may not have been possible. Publishing student writing is important not because students will get excited to see their words
in print, although that's true, but because students have beautiful and

important things to say to each other and the world (Students and Staff of the Open Book, 1991).

If people don't tell their own stories, hooks (1994) cautions, others do it for them. hooks adds, "there is no need to hear your voice when we can talk about you better than you can speak about yourself. I want to know your story. And I will tell it back to you in a new way. Tell it back to you in such a way that it has become my own. Re-writing you, I write myself anew. I am still author, authority, I am still the colonizer, the speaking subject, and you are now at the center of my talk. Stop" (pp. 151–152). Publishing oral histories is one way of preventing objectification; through people telling their own stories, they're defining their realities. They're subjects, authors, actors, instead of being the center of someone else's talk.

You have read examples of how students' voices were heard and reflected in the curriculum through co-writing a play and creating an oral history book together. In what other ways were students' voices reflected in how the program was shaped and structured? How was space fostered for this to happen? The next chapter explores one of the ways the Open Book attempted to do this.

FOUR

Hands Wash Hands but They Both Wash the Face

Students as Assistant Teachers

I would like to invite you to reflect on some of the following questions with me. I won't attempt to answer them here. I'm not entirely sure I can but they might give you a glimpse into some of the ways we as literacy workers collectively put our own philosophies and thinking under the microscope and were forever changed as a result (which meant the directions the program grew in were also affected).

I've been thinking a lot about the concept of making space for people and ideas as well as the connection between making space and different voices being heard and multiple realities being represented. Sissel and Sheared (2001) point out that when one is invisible, one does not take up space in our minds, our hearts, nor our economic, historical, political, or social concerns (p. 6). What does it then mean to make space for people and ideas? How is it possible? What would it look like? How do we make space for others in our lives, in our hearts, in our minds, in our communities, and in society? To what extent did it happen at the Open Book? Did we make space in the fullest ways we knew how? Whose voices was space being made for? If we only make space for people and ideas that reflect our own perspectives, how do we then ensure that the basic rights of everyone gain importance in the hearts and minds of the dominant culture? Space and meaning as forces are constantly shifting, being negotiated and renegotiated. Whose voices get to be included in discussions rooted in action and change? Whose voices get to ultimately be heard and listened to? How committed were staff and students at the Open Book to include the different voices that would foster more equitable and democratic options? To what extent was a collective dialogue started and how could it have been more fully realized in the context of the Open Book? Where were students' voices located in this conversation? To what extent was space being made for creating alternative power structures in classrooms and communities? What would that have looked like? These questions may seem overwhelming in their scope, yet these were just a few of the questions the staff at the Open Book grappled with at meetings and in informal conversations (and that continue to haunt me years later, long after the program has ended) as we sought to challenge our own thinking, our own ways of being in order to foster and ensure more inclusion, more voices, and more perspectives in the shaping of the program. Hiring assistant teachers was just one of the ways space was made at the Open Book.

In 1987 some students and teachers attended a conference at Lehman College (one of the City University of New York campuses in the Bronx). At this particular conference, one of the workshops presented by three assistant teachers from a community-based organization in the Bronx focused on the concept of implementing assistant teachers in an adult literacy program. Basemah and Deanna, two students from the Open Book, were audience members in the workshop and very excited about the idea of this being implemented at the Open Book. "Wow, let's do this" was their reaction. John went to his supervisor, who supported the idea, making available a small amount of funding, which made it possible to hire Deanna. Having an assistant teacher opened up a new set of possibilities in the program. She was able to work with students in ways the instructors weren't. Many students saw her as an insider in many of their own experiences; she had walked in shoes that reflected their own lived realities. This was especially true for one student, Ester, who could read the alphabet but not much more. She resisted the idea of writing, insisting she had nothing to say. However, Deanna was able to reach her almost from the very beginning. She was able to talk with her in a way that an instructor couldn't because she had been there herself. John's reflections below exemplify one way Deanna was able to impact the shape and direction of the class in ways an instructor couldn't.

John: One day I remarked to Deanna that I was unhappy with how the class was going. I felt people weren't very focused or into what we were doing. Deanna and Basemah [a student from Palestine who was active in a group for battered women and deeply committed to the idea of student participation] talked and decided to hold a meeting of the class without me. The next day they asked me if I would mind leaving the room for a while. I left and the class met together for about a half hour. I'm not sure what was said, but I think there was a clearing of the air. People spoke honestly about how they were feeling about the class and each other; they spoke in a way they wouldn't have if I were present. The meeting went really well, and I think surprised everybody how big a difference it made.

Deanna ended up working in the beginning class as an assistant teacher for two days, four hours each day. After she left the program, Basemah became the assistant teacher.

In the following conversation, which took place in 1994, Basemah and Cecilia, the counselor, reflect on their experiences of being assistant teachers (Cecilia, who is originally from Venezuela, also worked as a tutor) and what it meant for them, other students, and the program. Tragically, Basemah was killed in a car crash in May 2005. I had spoken with her once on her cellphone for a few minutes regarding her participation in this project. She was very interested but was in the middle of an appointment. We agreed to speak again soon. She was killed shortly afterward returning from Michigan after attending the opening of an Arab American museum there. She was a much loved, very important, and vibrant member of the Open Book community as well as an active and valuable presence in the Arab community in Brooklyn, New York.

*   *   *

Basemah: I am a student at the Open Book. I also work as an assistant teacher in the beginning class. I enjoy being an assistant teacher because I am more involved with the students. People trust me because I used to be a student in their class. They feel I am one of them and not an outsider. I was afraid to make mistakes and of how the class would feel about an assistant teacher making mistakes. But in time I learned how the students felt about me in the class. Then I felt comfortable. I don't think I have changed from this experience but my friends think I am different. They say I am more self-confident. I am proud of my work. I am proud of helping students. I am now more willing to go on with my own schooling.

Cecilia: One of the things I enjoy doing most at the Open Book is tutoring. It brings me close to the students and gives me happiness when they improve, no matter how minimal it is. Tutoring has been a great experience not only because I've been helpful to students, but most of all because they have been great tutors for me too. You could say our relationship is like the saying "Hands wash hands and both wash the face." Together we learned to spell words that were difficult for me too. One of the students will laugh every time he reads the word "ask" because in the beginning, he used to pronounce it "ax." I would ask him "to chop heads or wood?" So now he pronounces it right and laughs when he remembers. I can guess when he isn't sure about a word because he says it with a question, making it easy for me to correct it.

Tutoring has set my feet on the earth. I used to think that unless you were a teacher you couldn't teach. I was scared and insecure. I was stupid enough to believe I was the one imparting knowledge to others, and I would repeatedly ask myself: What am I going to teach? How am I going to start? With what? Then there comes this young woman into class and asks: "Are you the teacher?" "No. I was just 'tootooring' for the summer." "Oh, you are the tutor," she said with impeccable pronunciation. "Good," she went on, "let's sit and read then." From then on she took it into her hands to correct my pronunciation, making me repeat words until they sounded good to her. Here she was learning how to read with me, and at the same time she was instructing me in what I lack. What a humble experience this has been.

Basemah: The first two months were hard because I had my own problems with spelling. I would feel bad when I couldn't help students with their spelling. I used to think I couldn't do it. But in time with John and with the students' help, I was okay. Next year, I would like to get more involved with students after class. I also want to say that the meetings with John and the assistant teachers are very important. That's how I was able to have all the confidence and be strong: by asking John questions and listening to the other assistant teachers, what they have to say. We met weekly and we discussed how the class was going in general.

Cecilia: Teachers have a certain view of the world. They believe students' problems are caused by the system. Students often come from backgrounds where they had to abandon their education, but they don't blame the system; they blame themselves. "I can't learn." "I don't know what's wrong with me; I forget everything." "I fooled around too much." They can never pinpoint that when they went to school no one took time to encourage them or explain. It takes a long process to change them. There are sometimes years of humiliation students had to face.

Don't try to think you can understand students. That would be patronizing. Instead, spend more time with students, more close contact so you learn how to help them more directly. No matter how kind the teacher, a three-hour-a-day class can never be enough time. But the teacher getting more time with the student to deal with particular problems requires money.

The following conversation takes place among Aida, John, and Yolanda. Aida was a student who started at the program in 1991 in the beginning class and later became an assistant teacher in 1993. She was the assistant teacher until 2000. Yolanda started in the program as a student in 1986 and after obtaining her GED was hired as a part-time receptionist in 1988. She continued working as a receptionist for thirteen years. As in the preceding conversation, they reflect on the process of being hired as staff.

Aida: Students saw me as an equal. I was struggling the same way they were. In the beginning class we were all the same level and we knew each other's way of learning. When I was working with the students, I would wonder if I was doing the right thing. But the students helped me a lot. When it was time to read, I would sit down and read with them. If there was a word I couldn't figure out, I would tell the students, you know the word but I know the meaning of it. So we would discuss it and it would come popping into my head. They really helped me. I felt like they and I were learning together at the same time. And if they didn't like something they would tell me, they didn't hold back. I would say, "You have to stick with it, come back and work with us and we'll work with you." I felt like I reached inside and put a little bit of myself for them so they can reach out and say, "Well, I like it. I'm going to stay."

John: They felt comfortable with you. You really knew how to support people and I think that said something about the class as well. They were a very cohesive group.

Yolanda: I went to the Open Book basically looking to get my GED. It took me a while but I finally did get it. They had an opening for part-time receptionist and I remember Aida suggested, why don't you go for it? I was very nervous at the interview because I hadn't worked in quite some years. I was interviewed by John and a couple of other teachers. I think Aida and Corinne were there also.

John: We had some extra money, which is how we were able to do this. We interviewed at least one other person for the job.

Yolanda: After I got the job, it was different because I wasn't in tune with students as much. I was now on the outside. I wasn't as involved. But as time went on, I started getting closer to the students again. They started coming up and talking to me about their different problems. It felt good helping them out. I felt we all learned from each other. We not only learned from the teachers but we also learned from students. We all helped each other. In some way, we all contributed a little something to people's lives and I think that's what made it special. That's what I've held on to from the Open Book.

*   *   *

The idea of assistant teachers is not unique. The Open Book certainly didn't invent this concept but did implement it in a deep and committed way that made space for other sets of voices to be included in the ongoing conversation about the program. It's an important signifier because it does institutionalize the notion that students have important things to teach each other and everyone else. It honors them as knowledge creators and intellectuals in the learning process. It also gives concrete power to a group of students, which changes the dynamic of the program and opens up as well as establishes possibilities for teaching and learning to occur simultaneously.

• Basemah mentions the trust that other students had in her because she herself was a student in that particular class, and she knew what they were going through. Because she's a peer, students were willing to share with her in ways that could never be possible with an outsider (someone who's outside of their experiences and worlds). She had the capacity to understand their experiences because it may have mirrored her own in important ways. This notion of Basemah as a peer is also evident in the conversation Deanna and Basemah had with the students when John was asked to leave. The conversation that occurred in the room that day would have looked very different if John was sitting in the room. Because he was in a position of authority, students might have said very different things or may not have spoken at all. By John leaving the room, space was made for another type of conversation to occur.

• Hiring students as assistant teachers is an example of actions speaking louder than words—of, in a way, walking the talk. As Freire (1970) says, people need to experience and feel the difference, rather than just hear about it if their consciousness is to undergo an authentic change. While funding plays a central role in hiring students as assistant teachers, it's unclear that this is the sole factor at play. We, as literacy practitioners, must ask ourselves whether we're making space in every way we can, or are we gatekeepers and space-makers simultaneously? To what extent do people in positions of power inadvertently contribute to the powerlessness and disenfranchisement of students? Whom do we choose to let inside the gates? Whom do we keep out and further marginalize? I think if we truly wish to participate in a sustainable dialogue grounded in honesty and integrity that will move us forward as a field, we must be able to let light into all the dark and dusty rooms in our consciousness. We must be able to put our own assumptions under a microscope and scrutinize them. How are we complicit in benefiting from keeping the current structures intact? In maintaining the status quo and all the pain it inflicts on entire communities?

• One way we as instructors can inadvertently play the role of gatekeeper is by not recognizing students' knowledge as an essential component in the education process. Suppressing students' perspectives and voices from discussions will impact and shape what the program looks like and will affect the directions it will grow. Not hiring students is a basic way of not sharing power.

• Aida, Yolanda, and Cecilia all mention co-teaching/co-learning occurring simultaneously. Cecilia's example of working with a student who in turn worked with her on her pronunciation illustrates how assistant teachers are able to establish a relationship based on mutuality, on both of them being experts. This opens up possibilities for organic learning and peer teaching to occur on many levels. Freire (1970) says that we must work with people rather than working for or on them.

• Cecilia cautions against teachers' paternalism regarding students. Though well meaning, teachers can often feel protective of students and in doing this I believe there is the potential to create a relationship based on dependency, a benevolent colonization, where the instructor continues to be perceived as the expert, the holder of mysterious and omnipotent knowledge, instead of one where two people are seen as different but equal. Any serious hope of sustainability regarding shifts in power is greatly diminished by this stance.

• Cecilia mentions students' continuous self-blame in not succeeding in the school system. After all, how could teachers and all their aura of expertise be mistaken? So often students are made to feel the deficiency lies within them. This has certainly been my own experience of growing up in Guyana, South America, and for many years it was easier for me to believe that my own abilities were lacking. However, in my own process of unlearning, I understand more and more the different ways the system is deeply biased and doesn't have my best interests at heart (or those of other students who don't fit into the white, middle-class norm). This toxic message drilled into the consciousness of so many students is one of many urgent reasons to conduct power analyses in class with students, to critically analyze systems and other structures in society. As Cunningham (2000) asks, to what degree do we recognize the structure of the dominant society and its pressures to control us? And to what degree will we democratize our practice and challenge the marginalization of others? Who holds most of the power? If as a field we hope to work toward an alternative vision of society, then students sharing power with staff is an important step in that direction.

The next chapter focuses on some ways students shared power in the program in an effort to redirect or subvert the unidirectional flow that is privileged by dominant society.

FIVE

Let Students Drive the Vehicle!

Student Leadership, Power, and Decision-Making

This chapter focuses on decision-making at the Open Book and the space that was made for voices to enter and shape the conversation about the growth and direction of the program. Primarily, this section examines some of the committees and meetings in which decisions were made around important issues.

From almost the very beginning of the program, the students and instructors came together every month to have a conversation about how people were experiencing the school and what changes people would like to see implemented. (The day students and evening students met separately.) This monthly gathering was the beginning of program-wide town hall meetings. Some of the conversations focused on how things were going for people. How were classes? What were some things people would like to see happen in the program? Initially, John would write down some points he might have wanted to address. He then opened up the agenda, inviting others to add to it. These meetings provided an opportunity for people to take part in decisions affecting the program and for the staff to receive feedback on what they were doing. The success rate for these meetings was varied. There were instances when students seemed alight with ideas and enthusiasm and other times when the conversation felt forced and stilted. Though this format may not have worked especially well for students who weren't comfortable in large groups, who perhaps were concerned about how they might sound to others, or how others would perceive their ideas, it was the first time for many of the students in the program to be asked to share their opinions, where they were listened to and had their vision incorporated into conversations regarding the way the school was run. It was a heady invitation and an exciting time to be a member who was helping to shape the development of the Open Book community. Some people's comments are excerpts from earlier publications.

John: This is how we work at the Open Book. When we have important decisions to make, we bring them to the students. It's not always easier that way; sometimes it would be a lot quicker to have the teachers make the decisions or to make the decisions by myself. But we believe that in the long run decisions we make as a community will be the better ones.

Over time, new groups were formed by students. The women's group was started when one day Basemah approached John and told him she and a group of women students in the program needed to have a space to discuss issues as women. It wasn't a question, just a simple statement. So the women's group began meeting. This was an important group because it was very much an example of a group run by students for students; it was an idea that a group of students had that they themselves solely executed. The group met every Thursday in the library for seven months.

John: Basemah told me some of the women wanted to form a support group to talk about things that were going on for them as women.... Several of the women had already been in groups before that were run by social workers. Here they were looking for a place where they could give each other support as women. I think they felt like having a social worker run the group was like saying they couldn't take care of themselves. Even though the group didn't last ... it was an important milestone because it was the first time students had carried out a project on their own. They had begun to see the school as their space. In a way, it set the stage for things that came later on.

Rose Marie, one of the first students who attended the Open Book and who was a member of the women's group, reflects on why the group was important to her:

Rose Marie: I needed this bad. Your mind can't get set on school when you have so many problems in your own house. The group helped to relieve the anger, the tears, and the frustration in my life. I wished it lasted but some of the students just weren't taking it that seriously. They were always eating. I used to say to them, "Eat later. Let's talk about what's bothering us." But some of them continued fooling around. Finally I gave up and stopped going.

There was also a counseling group, which began when a group of students started meeting to discuss issues in their lives that were separate from the program. It was a space for people to meet and share on very deep levels in equally deep ways. People could share difficult and painful stories about their lives and families and knew that it would be safe with the other people in the room. A therapist had expressed interest in being invited to facilitate it as a volunteer. Her invitation was accepted and she began meeting with the students. Cecilia was the only staff member invited to attend. Whatever was discussed among the students was considered sacred by everyone who was a part of that group. The words remained locked inside their hearts and the room where meetings occurred.

Cecilia: My granddaughter started coming to the program and during one of the sessions I heard her talking about her mother for the first time. I had never touched those points before with her. When I heard her speak, I was shocked out of my wits. It was really quite intense. Other people talked about their former loves; about their lives.... It opened up everything because afterward we became closer.

Virginia: Those meetings seemed really important. I have no idea what went on in there because people were so good about the confidentiality but I know the atmosphere really changed in the school.

Then there was the student-teacher council. This new group consisted of a smaller group of people, so people who were less comfortable in large groups such as town hall meetings might find it easier for their voices to be heard. The council met on Saturdays, which provided an opportunity for both the day and evening students to meet each other and talk about strengths and weaknesses between the two.

John: The student-teacher council was a big step forward for the Open Book. It was the first time we had a group that really saw its job as thinking about the future of the school. We looked at the budget together, discussed problems that arose between students and teachers, made decisions on whether to buy math books or more literature. Whenever something important came up that needed to be addressed, that was definitely the place we did it.

Over the years, space was made for many more groups to be formed by students and teachers. The hiring committee was one such group. They consisted of a group of students and approximately two staff members who interviewed potential teaching candidates. Committee members received copies of résumés and would (if possible) meet before the interview. They would go over the résumé and talk about possible questions to ask each candidate. After the interview, they discussed their impressions of the candidate during the interview, their strengths, their weaknesses, and whether this would be a good fit.

In yet another important example about making space for voices to be heard, Virginia and John reflect on the first weekend retreat that was held in November 1990. This event not only supported students in thinking about more inclusive ways of decision-making but also was important in shaping the overall culture of the program. The entire weekend continued to be a powerful memory for people for many years. Dalita Guittierez, a program director from Chicago who had herself been a student in a community-based organization, facilitated this weekend retreat.

Virginia: I believe the retreats (and town hall meetings, committees) were an absolutely essential part of democratic decision-making. I remember one retreat in particular when Dalita Guittierez was one of our speakers for a weekend retreat. It was a two-day retreat (Saturday and Sunday) with lots of workshops, some that students facilitated with teachers. There was a lot of student support from the very beginning; it really wouldn't have gotten anywhere otherwise. For me, that was one of the main things that was special about the Open Book, helping people to say what they felt and to listen to what others have to say. It's not easy; I mean none of us are necessarily very good or practiced at it.

John: We saw the retreat as a time we could step back from our day-to-day work and think about the school. What were our goals as a community? What were the students' goals? What was working well and what was not working well? How would we change the school if we could? We invited Dalita Guittierez, director of a community-based program in Chicago, to lead the retreat. Dalita had been a student in an adult education program once herself so she had a feel for where the students were coming from. She began by telling everyone a little about herself: how she came to this country from Mexico not knowing how to read and write in English or Spanish; how she had enrolled in an adult education program; how one of the teachers had convinced her that she should become a tutor; how she eventually got her GED and started a new program in Chicago. Most of the students were amazed. She had come so far and accomplished so much. We spent part of the time with everyone meeting together and part with the students and teachers meeting separately. The teachers often meet by themselves, but it was a new thing for such a large group of students to meet on their own. It was important to give the students some time to really talk honestly among themselves and not worry or be afraid of hurting the teachers' feelings. And also to possibly work things out between themselves that sometimes they needed to work out.

And just like that morning when Deanna was still assistant teacher and the class asked me to leave so they could talk, this meeting turned out to be very positive. The students opened up in a way that they really didn't when the teachers are present, and Dalita helped them to see they could really have a big impact on the school if they wanted to. Just about everyone felt good about the retreat. The school community was renewed and strengthened by the experience, and some great ideas emerged from it.... Perhaps the most important one was the student-teacher council.

Virginia: I recall students being so impressed by Dalita's history. It was super inspiring; at least it was to me. That she could take her life to so many different places considering where she started from.

*   *   *

In the conversation below, John, Cecilia, and Earle reflect on the hiring committee, student-teacher council, town hall meetings, and the overall impact committee meetings had on the program. Earle was a student at the Open Book from 1995 to 2001. He very actively participated on many different levels in the program during the time he was there and began volunteering as the receptionist in the daytime when Yolanda (the permanent receptionist) was out. Eventually he was hired as the evening receptionist. He and another student coedited *The Gazette,* a student newspaper. He was also a participant on several committees. There are times when people refer to Eighth Street or Twelfth Street in their conversations. For the first eleven years, the Open Book was located on Fifth Avenue at the corner of Eighth

Street in Brooklyn. In 1996, the program moved to Twelfth Street, also at the corner of Fifth Avenue in Brooklyn.

* * *

Earle: For me, being a student at the Open Book was very empowering. We not only learned reading and math but advocacy like understanding the system and learning to stand up and fight for what we believed in. It's like being given the keys to a whole different learning spectrum. It wasn't just a place where you just sit in a classroom but a place where you can be a leader. I was given the opportunity to really be a voice of the school, to put together events and bring it back to meetings. An example would be the leadership class which I was a part of. We would decide certain things that were going on within the school.

John: From almost the very beginning there were different ways for people to participate. We had a student-teacher council meeting once a month, which was a really important idea from students. Up until then, the main way students participated in decision-making in the school was through town hall meetings, which we had once a month. But some people saw those as limited. They were very big and discussion wasn't always very focused. While they were effective for putting ideas on the table, getting feedback, etc., we needed more. Students wanted to have a stronger voice. So we decided to form a group of students and teachers that would be the final decision-making body for the school. It met once a month on a Saturday so both evening and day students could participate. They were open to any students and staff who wanted to come and ideally should have had at least two students from each class. While attendance was a struggle, a lot of people felt this was a big success. We also had town hall meetings approximately once a month where we'd bring classes together. In the early years I would lead the meetings. I would come in with some things that I wanted to talk about and then open it up for other people to suggest things. But then over at Twelfth Street students began running the meetings.

Cecilia: Earle, I remember when you first came to the program. You were very shy. On your first day, do you remember, how you told me someone from the neighborhood was bothering you and you wanted me to write a letter for you? And I said, believe me, you're going to write that letter yourself.

Earle: I was really nervous that day. I had just come from another program where they weren't as kind or as understanding. There teachers abused their powers against other people and you couldn't speak up. Who's going to believe one person over this teacher that's got so much clout? One teacher smacked me in my face because I wrote something she didn't like and that was how she retaliated. Anyway, when I got to the Open Book there was a vision and everyone's involvement just added to the vision.

John: I remember you and other students being involved in the class schedule being changed from nine hours a week to sixteen hours. We used to meet for three hours a day, three days a week, but students pushed for more hours. We brought the three classes together and had meetings around it. In most of the other programs the teachers and directors decide what the program is going to look like. But here students initiated it.

Earle: It wasn't just a staff school; it was for students and staff. We all had a hand in creating the Open Book. It wasn't Cecilia's school or John's school. Everybody had a piece of the Open Book pie. That's something schools don't do. Nobody did what we did. Nobody came even close!

Cecilia: I think the students really recognized that it wasn't a rigid program. It was a place for them to develop and to make their own. John doesn't like to take credit but I see this as a dream of his that this program should be this way. So he made room for it. He took on all of the heavy problems and allowed what happened at the program to develop. He held the Open Book together.

John: I'm not sure I agree with that. My role was fairly complicated. I agree with what Earle just said. It was everybody's creation. I did in a way make room/space for it. I did protect it, allow it to happen ... but I didn't make it happen. I made space but what it became was the result of everybody's contribution, especially students. They made a huge contribution.

Cecilia: I don't know anyplace where students can go to the director of the program and say we need a support group and the director will say, "Okay let's do it. Let's allow it to happen." But here we said, "Okay, let's see what other students think about it. Let's call everybody together." Then we would get together and there would be a discussion about it. That doesn't happen in other places.

John: I think what tends to happen in other programs is that directors might say "okay," but then they implement something that's not exactly what the students want, something they can control.

Cecilia: I remember, years ago, one teacher interviewed with us. She had come from another program. She told me after the interview that she was so scared to work in a place like this because she had never been interviewed by students anywhere she went.

Earle: Staff and students would come together as one entity to make a decision on who we think would fit in our community. I was never involved in a process like that before in my entire life in all the schools. I've never even heard this being done before. The person would come in and we sat them down. Each student got a chance to ask the candidate questions, different scenarios. Once the person left we would go back and talk about it, compare notes with each other, etc.

John: It was always a toss-up who was more nervous—the students or the person being interviewed. One thing I learned from students being involved in hiring was that it really helped the class think more carefully about what should be happening in the classroom and about their role in the process. Students gained a lot of confidence by participating, by getting the opportunity to ask questions of someone with a college degree. They saw they could do it and do it well.

Cecilia: I thought that was one very important part to the program. Students felt such importance to be able to participate like that. They felt it showed a respect for them because they got to choose their teachers. It wasn't imposed on them like in other programs.

Earle: Student involvement in the program was very extensive. Students wanted to see changes. We asked people what they thought about things, how this work would and how it wouldn't work, and how it would serve all of us and be better for all of us.

John: I remember also that on Twelfth Street the students started evaluating teachers. I think you were involved in coming to us and saying the students should have a chance to evaluate the teachers.

Earle: Well, we wanted to sum up the year. Did it work well for us? What could be better in the school? How many times do you go into a classroom and see students sitting in a classroom, but how many of them really connect with the teacher? Do they find their teacher boring or appealing? I think I posed the idea first to John and we brought it into a student meeting and I asked students what they thought about it. Students agreed. They said they liked the idea.

John: Then the group worked on developing some questions. The teacher left the room and the assistant teachers came into the classes and led the process. I think there was a sense for students that they had a voice here. Having a chance to talk about the teachers without them present was really important. It was an example, a kind of model. When you open up space for students to play a strong role and to organize, it opens up possibilities for tensions among the students. It's no different than anywhere else. There might have been people who were resentful of the role Earle played in the school.... I think it's one reason that administrators use for not allowing more autonomous organizing by students.

Earle: When you're trying to do something that would benefit the community sometimes people get resentful. You try to make them understand you're not here to control everything. There were a handful of students who felt their ideas weren't heard or who didn't say much. I would say well, what do you think? What do you have to say? What do you think the issues are? But sometimes people get lost in the mix or something gets miscommunicated.

John: I think this question of jealousies and the dynamics between students when they start organizing on their own is complicated. When you have a lot of people in the school who have never really had an opportunity to play leadership roles, tensions can develop. This is what made the Open Book special. Students had a chance to develop their ideas and talk, knowing they were respected. So when people have this opportunity for the first time, sometimes it feels good to them, this newfound confidence, and that can feed the jealousies. I think you just have to let it happen, try to provide some support for people, give students support in thinking through these kinds of problems that go with the territory. It's not smooth. When people are critical of Earle, he needs to be able to listen to that and say is that real or not? I'm not sure we did the best at really helping people think through those issues. There was a citywide student organization that Basemah was involved in right from the beginning. In some ways an organization like that could help people negotiate some of these problems. It's difficult for me to be in that role; I'm not really a peer. Overall it worked well but there were conflicts and tensions between students. I take it as a given that we could have done better. But I think the Open Book was a very open, welcoming community and didn't necessarily demand a lot of people to participate. You could participate intensely like Earle or not. Students had that choice. I think most people felt good about the choices we made as a program. So I don't really have any second thoughts about the model we developed, keeping in mind that we could always have done better.

Earle: I would like to encourage teachers and directors in literacy programs to listen to students. It is very important to listen to what they say and allow them to be innovative, to be themselves, to grow as people, to be an entity, to be part of something that could be great if you just allow it to happen. Let students drive the vehicle.

Cecilia: The thing that should be taken from the Open Book was the love that people put into it and that could be copied. It's not complicated to put your heart into something. Let your brain and heart work together but let your love be the construction of the dream. For me the Open Book didn't end. As long as one student benefited from the program, it's still living.

* * *

From the preceding conversation among John, Cecilia, and Earle, one can sense the program's commitment to exploring different ways of sharing power. Through town hall meetings, students were invited to envision a dream, take aspects of that dream, and incorporate those parts into the growth of the program. Students were also encouraged to assume leadership roles and practice the skills required for those roles. One example mentioned by John was how, in later years, students began leading the town hall meetings.

In this model, there was an underlying assumption that people learned new things by doing them, trying them out, experimenting with ways they could work, and then refining that vision. Students weren't only reading about issues in class but space was made in the program to develop as leaders. Freire (1970) reminds us that to exist humanly is to name the world, to change it. Once named, the world in its turn reappears to the namers as a problem and requires of them a new naming. Saying that word is not the privilege of a few, but the right of everyone (p. 76).

• As John mentioned, actual changes resulted from students' input. One example was the class schedule increasing from nine to sixteen hours. While it is obvious that funding plays a significant role in this decision, there is something else going on. Students are invited to envision and ponder ways the program could be more of a reflection of what they want. John listened to that and armed with that knowledge, pushed the envelope of democracy to lobby for students' wishes becoming a reality. There were inevitable limitations to this. Good Shepherd, the Open Book's umbrella agency, almost certainly wasn't open to all of the requests of the staff and students, but the pockets of possibility that did exist were seized upon.

• Is what occurred at the Open Book the result of one person's vision or that of a collective, one that wouldn't have been possible without everyone's contributions? This was an ongoing thread throughout discussions surrounding this project. There are differences of opinions around this issue. Cecilia perceives John's role as being the stalk from which leaves grew but John downplays this analysis. As the central figure of authority, John undeniably shaped the culture in terms of being one of the main space-makers of possibilities by inviting students to inhabit that space with him and other staff members. As a result, students filled the space he (and others) created and protected with their determination, courage, and love to form a brilliant, multicolored mosaic, each color blending with the next until where one ended and the next began was no longer visible—entirely new colors formed. In certain ways, it seems to me, both Cecilia and John are correct in parts of the analysis. If administrators didn't foster space and encourage students to push the envelope to realize there was a problem, then any potential conversation would have reached an abrupt halt. But if the administration fostered space and that invitation wasn't answered by extraordinary students filling the canvas with brilliant storied colors of their lived realities, then the canvas would have remained sterile and blank. There was a third scenario as well. The ways that students made space for possibility. What doors did they force open? To what extent did they push back on the administration? Evidence of this could be glimpsed in Earle's and other students' request to evaluate instructors.

• The concept of power is multilayered. Like an unseen guest, it is ever present, taking a seat in the room, inserting itself in our actions, our attitudes, and our everyday lives. If it's always present, then one is never outside it. Each of us not only is affected and shaped by the flow of power, but we each also affect and shape this flow (Brookfield, 2005). At the Open Book, alternative decision-making structures affecting the flow of power were put in place, to support people in realizing that their voices and perspectives mattered; they mattered.

• Students like those at the Open Book exist in every literacy program yet they were able to accomplish things and impact the landscape of the program in important ways. If space is made and protected in other programs, isn't it likely that magical possibilities could also open up? Why then isn't this happening in other programs? What prevents it from becoming a reality? Is it about controlling students? Not wanting them to share power, voice, or knowledge? Who benefits from things staying the same and not changing? As Morley and Worpole (2010) say, the questions of who is to speak, who is to be listened to, and what kinds of voices and ways of writing are to be valued are always questions of political power (p. 116).

• I recall working in another literacy program (after the Open Book had closed). During our first town hall meeting, students' suggestions ranged from different paint colors for the walls to changing the chairs. No one suggested anything more than changing the décor of the program. Finally one student said, "No one ever asked us what we wanted before. How do we know you're really going to listen? Why should we tell you?" Initially, students may not be willing to share. After all, how do they really know nonstudents have their best interests at heart? Earle's instructor at the Department of Education (the adult education component of the public education system that runs grades K–12) certainly didn't appear to. But the experience of students at the Open Book suggests that when people feel an integrity and sincerity in those invitations, they may be more willing to answer that invitation. However, I would like to forewarn that if this is just an exercise in lip service on the part of the administration, if there isn't sufficient dedication and commitment to embark on this exciting adventure where the road is made by walking, I believe the process and outcome will be ultimately shallow—a pale and brittle version of what could be.

• As we saw from the preceding conversation, this model will most likely be very difficult to implement in other programs without the support from the administration. If directors don't make the space, or aren't fully committed to this, the endeavor will most likely perish in its embryonic stages. John speculates about program directors adapting students' requests and implementing a version of those they can control. What is so threatening about students sharing power? What are the broader implications of this? Why doesn't it happen more often? Cecilia says that at the heart of the Open Book was love and that could be implemented elsewhere. Why isn't it? Why aren't students a part of the process of interviewing and hiring instructors? Mightn't there be a greater chance of the most suitable candidate being hired? By students collectively working on developing and refining interview questions, aren't they working on reading and writing proficiency ... reading and writing the world, their community, what it needs, and who might best fill that? An opportunity to be authors of a script?

• This shift in power and the ways it gets played out is often invisible. How is this rerouting of power perceived by other students? If a few students' ideas keep getting heard, does that signal to other students that these ideas are "superior"? How does this affect the landscape of this newly formed settlement where space and voice play vital roles? How are the quieter voices affected by this? Was the space dominated by the most articulate voices with the most clearly shaped ideas or were there visible access points for others to enter? In a seemingly more equitable and inclusive environment is the old order of competitions and rewards of the dominant culture of schooling inadvertently being re-created? This multilayered issue is ever present, and

I believe it is important for people to be attentive so the dominant ways of schooling and culture aren't being reproduced, albeit in a new suit with a possible facelift. For the students, like Earle, it can be a heady feeling to be listened to in a serious way and to bask in the approval of your ideas by others. This might be difficult to resist after years of invisibility in school. Who are the oppressed and the oppressors? Is there the capacity in ourselves and students to be simultaneously both? To play the role of oppressor after being oppressed by the dominant system for so long? I would argue that the harm inflicted on each of our psyches by this culture goes to our core, seeps deep into our consciousness, is internalized, and can emerge in harmful ways if not critically examined. Weiler (1988) says that there is a capacity within each of us to adopt this oppression and consciously or unconsciously adapt it in other contexts. In each of us lies the capacity to play many roles—the community activist and abusive partner. Bannerji (2002) writes about the process of discovering oppression in all its complexity. Multiple social group memberships can sometimes be fragmented and contradictory (Usher, Bryant, and Johnston, 1997).

Changing practices does not do away with power but instead can reconfigure it. Foucault (1977) points out that the place from which power is exercised is often hidden. "When we try to pin it down, the center always seems to be somewhere else. Yet we know that this phantom center, elusive as it is, exerts an undeniable power over the whole social framework of our culture and over the ways that we think about it.... It defines the tacit standards from which specific others can then be declared to deviate, and while that myth is perpetuated by those whose interests it serves, it can also be internalized by those who are oppressed by it" (p. 9). Were we at the Open Book inadvertently privileging certain skill sets over others? Is it ever possible not to? Even when we understand how deeply the dominant system has harmed us in ways both seen and unseen, it's the only model most of us have ever been exposed to; it's the only compass many of us have. Understanding that something is not in our best interests doesn't automatically stop us from believing in it, from ejecting it from our consciousness (Martin, 2001). How then can we negotiate this treacherous terrain? Hart (2001) says that to remap or countermap means to acknowledge, learn about, and attempt to understand the many different struggles of many different groups of people to survive, to resist or battle against the onslaught of injustice and destruction, and to gain or regain some power over their lives in a way that acknowledges the dignity of life in all its forms. She adds that in order to be able to do this, we must be able to be silent, to listen and observe, to open ourselves up for critique, and to make ourselves vulnerable (pp. 180–181). We have to engage in developing our own version of a mestiza consciousness. John, in recognizing that he can never be an insider in this conversation, suggests supporting students in thinking through some of these murky issues. Maybe role-playing could be one way of critically analyzing dominant models of leadership as a way of making transparent the qualities they privilege. John also suggests that connecting with student-led organizations can support emerging student leaders in analyzing this rocky and sometimes slippery slope. Were there areas where we could have been more effective? As John points out, yes, things could always have been improved, done differently.

• Let students drive the vehicle! The challenges to be negotiated should never be enough of a factor to put the brakes on fostering student involvement regarding all decisions that are made affecting the program. Their voices should guide us through this terrain. Cunningham (2000, p. 584) invites the field to recognize that all persons are knowledge creators and that by working within social movements we are provided with opportunities to re-create our definition of adult education, one that reclaims our history.

• In the preceding conversation around the weekend retreat with Dalita, Virginia points out that the Open Book community really practiced articulating and listening to others' ideas, something we in society are rarely given the opportunity to do. In that statement, she uses the word "we." There is recognition that teachers are included in this, not as the all-knowing experts, but that they too are engaged in their own struggles (though these struggles might look very different from students').

• In inviting Dalita to lead the retreat, there is a cognizance of outsiderness/insiderness to the extent that it is ever possible for us to be insiders to each other's experiences. Certainly, Dalita had much more insight into students' experiences than instructors ever could and there was recognition by instructors that their presence would almost certainly inhibit conversation. But I wonder whether people's experiences are really ever knowable to others? (Ellesworth, 1989).

The next chapter problematizes a major issue that impacted adult literacy students at the Open Book and elsewhere in the mid-1990s. The issue of literacy workers' possible inadvertent complicity in maintaining the status quo regarding structural systems we might be philosophically opposed to is also raised and unpacked.

Six

What About Students' Rights to Dignity, Autonomy, and Respect?

The Welfare Battle

The president keeps repeating the "dignity of work" idea. What dignity? Wages are the measure of dignity that society puts on a job. Wages and nothing else. There is no dignity in starvation. Nobody denies, least of all poor women, that there is dignity and satisfaction in being able to support your kids through honest labor. We wish we could do it. If I were president, I would solve this so-called welfare crisis in a minute and go a long way towards liberating every woman. I'd just issue a proclamation that "women's" work is real work. I'd start paying women a living wage for doing the work we are already doing—child raising and housekeeping. And the welfare crisis would be over, just like that.

—Johnnie Tillmon, 1972

So far the story has focused on the internal life of the Open Book, but this chapter switches to the external context of the field. The struggles occurring during this period had a deep impact on the everyday life of the Open Book. In the mid-1990s storm clouds were brewing over New York City and the rest of the country in the form of the welfare battle and adult literacy students' right to attend education programs. The Welfare Literacy Coalition, a group of teachers, students, and program directors, began organizing, holding meetings around the issue. This group was formed as a response to welfare policy's impact on literacy programs in New York City. Several important grassroots actions emerged from those meetings. There was a

Day of Action on Welfare Rights, which focused on increasing funding for adult education programs that students from the Open Book were involved in. In the spring of 1995 there was a dramatic speak-out at New York City Technical College, one of the City University of New York campuses in Brooklyn. Droves of students and instructors showed up to this event full of passion and anger against what they perceived to be the blatant injustice of policies surrounding welfare reform.

Some of the source of this outrage was rooted in how students on public assistance were being treated. Welfare reform laws mandated that students attend classes a certain amount of hours per week and work the remainder of the time. In 1996, students on public assistance were required to attend literacy programs twenty hours a week in order to continue receiving their benefits. Then, President Clinton in the Welfare Reform Act of 1996 stated that, in effect, students didn't need to attend classes—they just needed to work if they were to continue receiving their benefits. As Gordon (2000) stated, en masse, literacy programs lost a key part of their student body as welfare recipients were forced out of school and into workfare programs. We were told that we had to cut our classes to no more than fifteen hours a week so welfare recipients would have time to clean the streets. It felt a bit like literacy was the tail being wagged by welfare policy.

Any pretense that education played a vital role was quickly dispelled. At the Open Book, students who were on public assistance were forced to leave the program and work in welfare employment programs in order to maintain their paltry checks. However, there were some students whose schedules permitted them to switch to evening classes. There were a series of meetings that Open Book students and teachers attended. A significant core of the New York City literacy community was engaged in what many saw as a clear infringement of students' basic rights. One of the options considered by government funders during this time was installing a telephone in literacy classrooms; students who were on public assistance would need to call in so funders could be assured that students were indeed attending class. In other words, staff in literacy programs were being enlisted to police the students.

In the following excerpt of an article, which appeared in slightly different form in *Literacy Harvest* (Winter 1995), John Gordon reflects on the effect of this policy on the Open Book and examines the implications of the roles literacy workers were forced to adopt in this process. (To read the entire article, please see Appendix D.)

* * *

The Walls of My Mind
Andrea Ortiz

The walls of my tired mind
Afraid to support another war
Cracking and seeing the time pass by
Shadows of mystery behind
Too old to choose where to go
Cemetery's lonely bodies unknown
Feels strong not to fold
Until I'm crossing to see another
world.

Many of us came into adult education because we believed in the transformative power of adult education, because we believed that learning to read and write would not just open doors for some individuals but had the potential to give students the skills to understand and act on their world more effectively, to gain control over their lives, to act in concert with others to change the conditions of life in their communities. Implicit in this view was a notion that education itself was good, that by learning to read people would be opened up to new experiences and ideas, and in the process become different and perhaps more powerful people....

I think that this belief in the potential of education to sponsor and provoke change, rather than the hope that we could help them get jobs (no matter how important that is), is what inspired many of us to become teachers. This article is about the way welfare is transforming the nature of literacy and English as a Second Language classes in the city. But it is also about us—teachers, administrators, counselors—and our role in this process. It is about what we want to be doing and what we are doing.

Five years ago, the Office of Employment Services (OES) began to demand that Adult Basic Education (ABE) programs report student attendance. About once a month, OES sends each program a roster of its students on Public Assistance known to be receiving Training Related Expenses (TREs). TREs include transportation, childcare, and sometimes lunch money. Programs are expected to report on the attendance of the students listed in order to determine whether or not they should continue receiving TREs....

When at the Open Book we first began to receive the roster, it led us to reflect on a number of things. First and foremost was the question of how to respond so that students would not be hurt. Second, we wondered where it fit into impending welfare reform legislation. What would be required of programs and of recipients in the future? It led us to also reflect upon our role as educators. Most of us receive funding and support from institutions whose goals sometimes contradict our own. How do we respond to the demands of those institutions and still remain accountable to ourselves and to students? Who is to determine what we do when faced with this contradiction? As teachers and administrators, we realize that we have a responsibility to continually question whom we are actually serving. We have to challenge ourselves or fall victim to the bureaucracies that attempt to dictate to us and our students....

Central in this discussion is the issue of trust. Most ABE students have had a difficult time in past school experiences and almost all bring with them a profound sense of alienation from and mistrust of the education system. Programs that have been successful in attracting and retaining students have been able to establish an atmosphere of warmth and support, allowing students to feel free to expose their weaknesses, and where relationships of trust and confidence can grow among the students, staff, and teachers' relationships that are able to break down that sense of alienation and mistrust that tends to govern relations between people and the institutions that "serve" them.

Our feeling is that if we took on the role of monitoring student attendance and if our reports could result in loss of benefits, we could be undermining the very relationships that we have worked so long and hard to build. People would begin to see us as a police arm of welfare, and their presence in class as coerced. Under these circumstances, many might not remain, and those that did might not trust enough to learn.

We were troubled at what appeared to be acceptance of this policing role on the part of other programs. Was it because people were too busy with other things to deal with this? Did others not see the broader implications of these rosters? Was there a sense of powerlessness among educators in the face of the massive welfare bureaucracy? Was everyone just planning to lie? ...

On top of this, BEGIN programs were now in existence, specifically for students on public assistance. Some community-based organizations, as well as the City University system, are running their own BEGIN programs, which further ghettoize welfare recipients. Their entrance into the program, their attendance, and departure are coerced....

All of these developments take place in a climate in which welfare recipients are increasingly being cast as scapegoats. President Clinton has made welfare reform one of the central tenets of his program. It is Clinton, in fact, who has given legitimacy to the notion that people should only be on welfare for two years. Here in New York City, Mayor Giuliani, by demanding that public assistance recipients be fingerprinted, has set the stage for a kind of criminalization of people on welfare.

Students have reacted angrily to these developments. At the Open Book, many students talked about the way they are mistreated by the welfare system, that "just because they give you some money they think they can run your life." They felt it was ridiculous to expect someone to gain proficiency in a language or become a good reader in two years. One student at the Open Book had this reaction. "Why don't they just put those ankle bracelets on you, like the ones they use for people on house arrest? Then they'll always know where we are."

Students in five or six programs organized meetings in their schools and traveled to other boroughs to hold joint meetings. In those meetings they came up with three demands: no time limits on participation to adult education programs, no more rosters, no unannounced visits by the State Department of Social Services.

We tend to regard welfare's demands as an unwelcome intrusion into the educational process, but for funders and policy-makers they are part of the same package. Whatever our intentions are, literacy funding is primarily directed not at providing people with an education but at getting people off the welfare rolls. It is aimed not so much at education, but at re-education; not so much at giving people the academic and intellectual tools they need to better control their destiny, to understand and deal with the society we live in, but rather to change their attitudes, to convince them that they have no choice but to take a job, no matter how bad, no matter how low-paying, no matter how personally unfulfilling.

Many students could go out and get a minimum wage job at McDonald's or some other such place, but they do not. Why? Because the jobs are degrading, because there would be no health insurance, because they are smart enough to know that for them it does not pay. People resist bad choices. The function and purpose of adult literacy funding is, more than anything else, to break down that resistance. This direction, this orientation in literacy policy has been straightforward, out in the open and clearly stated for a long time.

The worst part about it is that we in the adult education community have not only acquiesced to these developments, we have accepted the basic assumptions behind welfare reform and incorporated them into our curricula and program designs. We have become cops for the welfare system.

The only protest I have heard with any consistency is about the amount of time and effort that goes into filling out forms and other types of paperwork. Some have argued that we should demand to be paid for this time.

I agree there is an enormous amount of time wasted in filling out these forms, but I think if our strategy is to ask to be paid for the time, we, in essence, buy into the system. We put our stamp of approval on it; in fact we begin to benefit from it because our salaries will then be paid partly by these funds. And this is the problem—our reactions to the encroachments of welfare have been shaped and conditioned by our positions as administrators, teachers, and counselors. We see the issues from the perspective of people who are inside the system and have a stake in its continuance, rather than from the perspective of the people who are outside, the students themselves.

The logic of the debate is always set by the needs and prerogatives of the system itself. The government insists that if it is going to be paying out millions of dollars every year in carfare and childcare expenses, then it has the right to make sure that the money is being spent where it is supposed to be. Well, yes. But then again, what about the students' perspective? What about their right to respect, dignity, and autonomy?

I would argue that these funding initiatives and welfare reforms are inherently oppressive, designed to regain control over a workforce that is, in a certain sense, in rebellion. How many of the people who are in the BE-GIN program would really rather not be there? For that matter, how many public assistance recipients in the other ABE and English Speakers of Other Languages (ESOL) programs would rather not be there? I do not pretend to know the answers to those questions, but I do think that if the answer is "a lot," then these programs would be better off closed.

... My purpose is not to attack. These are confusing issues, and the alternatives are not all that clear. But I think we all need to take a good hard look at what we are doing. We need to think not only about what adult education is, but what it is in the process of becoming. From the point of view of students on public assistance, how much difference is there between BEGIN and another program? How much difference will there be in a year?

We need to listen to the students. We need to develop some unity around these issues. We need to figure out how we can have an impact on literacy policy. We have to expand our focus from "how much" to "what" and "why." And we have to make some choices.

*   *   *

John raises many questions that are problematic about welfare reform's impact on literacy students. He emphatically stated, "We have to make some choices." The article was written in 1995, yet in a metaconversation, in so many ways, the issues look very similar in 2011. Students' voices still go unheard (or unlistened to) by policy-makers and many members of the field are still engaged in the backbreaking collective struggle to blow the wind in another direction. In the same vein of the preceding excerpt, I'd like to add some of my own reflections and raise some further questions.

• In underscoring John's point about programs' complicity in assuming a murkier role in students' miseducation, I would ask how can we as literacy workers expect to enter a relationship with people built on trust and integrity when we're enlisted to spy on them? To act in concert with the very systems we may wish to subvert or disrupt? How can people be vulnerable and open with teachers and with each other if there is even a threat of suspicion that the information may be used against them? Yet isn't this exactly what funders force upon education programs with every new initiative or reform? How can welfare benefits (which are well below the poverty line) be justified as anything other than a Band-Aid solution (and an ineffective one)—another attempt at making poor people scapegoats in an economic system that cares best for its most powerful, least vulnerable members?

• When someone constantly checks up on you, there's usually an assumption that you're not trustworthy. As Ehrenreich (2001, p. 210) states, America can hardly pride itself on being the world's preeminent democracy, after all, if large numbers of its citizens spend half of their waking hours in what amounts to a dictatorship that takes its psychological toll on its subjects. If you're repeatedly treated as untrustworthy, you may begin to feel untrustworthy yourself. If you're constantly bombarded with messages of your inferior social position, you begin to eventually accept your status without question, accept that one group's socially constructed version of reality of your status must be correct and has more value attached to it. One instructor from the Open Book stated that one of the main principles embedded in the program was a basic assumption that people were good and worthy of trust.

• How do we then as literacy workers reconcile what we know to be true through our lived realities that adult literacy is grounded in and intimately connected to larger issues surrounding institutionalized social inequities, marginalization, and further oppression? (Stuckey, 1991; Macedo, 1994). How do we go on when policy-makers' visions, which privilege discrete skills, actually de-skill, anesthetize, and deaden the spirit? Inherent in this prescriptive model is the assumption that one group of people knows what's best for another segment of society. As Freire (1970) stated, education either domesticates or liberates. Education either supports the status quo or challenges it. There is no middle ground.

• Aren't welfare reforms really about perpetuating a human underclass? After all, plenty of poor people who need work ensure cheap labor and, inevitably, exploitation. With so many people, working class and middle class alike, struggling to find gainful employment, whose economic interests are served (or not) by the inclusion of all this new labor in the workplace? By channeling welfare recipients (many of whom happen to be literacy students) into low-paying, dead-end jobs, isn't the government supplying the market with low-skilled labor while at the same time lowering wages for working-class people who are employed? (Kingfisher, 1996). It's a lose-lose situation for everyone involved (well, not quite everyone). We must be attentive to the insidious ways class systems are acted and reenacted every day. All social inequities in capitalist societies are fundamentally rooted in economic exploitation (Nesbit, 2004). Shouldn't someone be asking whether one group of people ever has the right to decide the ceiling of another person's dream, to decide what's best for another community? For one to imagine he or she can define and solve the problem of others has the overwhelming stench of paternalistic colonization (Memmi, 1965). Who benefits? Where is the reciprocity in this process? Isn't welfare an example of one of the many deeply entrenched barriers firmly blocking the students' path forward? According to Nesbit (2004), by transmitting, sustaining, and legitimizing particular systems of structured inequality, educational systems uphold the characteristics of a particular order of social relations. Such choices always benefit and privilege some while further depriviledging others (p. 19).

• What is our role as educators? Is it to zip students through classes, fill out necessary paperwork, and whisk them off to the workforce? Or is it something deeper? Something more intangible and complicated that touches both the head and the heart? Something more joyous and yet at times painful? A process that involves working with students for as long as it takes to support their growth and goals? As John asks, what happens when programs receive funding from institutions with goals that contradict their own? Isn't it possible that we may be contributing (however unintentionally) to people's further marginalization and oppression in fulfilling the demands of funders? Certainly there isn't any apparent space on funders' checklists for effecting change in communities. In fact, I would argue that under the current policy, it's strongly discouraged. Instead the focus is on raising students' reading level (as solely defined by standardized tests) so they can enter the workforce as soon as possible. Do this or be defunded. The choice is clear, the consequences stark. Many literacy workers will clearly say they're not interested in sacrificing standards. What they will say though is that they want the standards that are used to measure programs in meaningful ways, to capture the multiple stories grounded in everyday struggles and victories that capture students' strengths and progress in multifaceted, holistic, and humane ways. We need to think about what some of those ways would look like. In the current scenario, the deck is overwhelmingly stacked against programs.

• As literacy workers, many of us believe that inherent in the definition of literacy is a necessity to read the world so that people can transform society and have a better life, and that outsiders know nothing about what's best for communities (but certainly a lot about what's not). Is it any surprise that smaller, community-based programs get asphyxiated by the many strings involved in funding? In being pulled like marionettes in multiple and, at times, completely contradictory ways by opposing forces? It seems that in this current climate, literacy programs that are considered quality programs are the ones that have mastered jumping through the most institutionalized hoops. One tends to wonder whether the system, upheld by well-intentioned people (who are complicit whether they realize it or not), isn't working to further alienate already oppressed communities. If there's an invisible steel door that's being clanged shut, who's closing it? Who's being locked inside? What is education currently being used for? By whom?

• John raises the central issue of complicity, saying that we need to challenge ourselves and continually question whom we're serving. I question whether we have been strategic enough at locating spaces in which pockets of resistance could grow. What would this resistance look like? What qualities would be needed for those spaces to thrive and be sustained? Is it futile to believe that the literacy field can maintain autonomy in the face of this massive and dangerous hypocrisy we label a system? Is it to be the case where educators and students who stand up and acknowledge the inequities and hypocrisy of the system are left bloodied and clawing to stay alive and function? I believe we are, all of us, guilty of upholding the current system that we philosophically rail against and all that it promotes. After all, don't our salaries come from keeping the system intact in one form or another? As John points out, we need to think carefully about our choices. What exactly are the options open to us? His article was written in 1995. What has changed since then? I would argue that while the actors and specific issues might be different, there is still a struggle for the most basic of human rights to be implemented in our society. I believe we need to envision clear alternatives rooted in equality and equity for everyone and we must be willing to give up our privilege and complicity in this process. We must remember that lasting social change comes about through people acting together (Nesbit, 2004). We must be able to collectively frame the debate in ways that create alternative power structures and that remove most of the power from government, funders, and other gatekeepers who always seem to be the ones who have and hold on to power. That dynamic must shift, power must find its way to the people who suffer under the current structures now—namely, students who are disenfranchised and marginalized by the dominant culture.

What about when there is perceived infringement of those basic rights by the very same people who are perceived as space-makers? What about other roads that could have been traveled by us sojourners at the program? Chapter 7 explores the possibility of taking alternative routes and reflects on what those may have looked like.

Seven

Letting the Powers That Be to Be

One of the unique qualities of the Open Book was the space made for critical reflection. We used a portion of each staff meeting to talk about our work. Others would question, nudge, or gently probe to support the person speaking in clarifying his or her own thinking, seeing what happened from multiple perspectives, or just delving deeper into his or her own consciousness. Brookfield (1995) points out that by opening our teaching to colleagues we can notice aspects of our practice that were previously hidden from us. As peers and colleagues describe their readings of and responses to situations and ethical dilemmas we face, we're able to see our practice and classrooms in new ways. In essence, shining a light on areas regarding our practice for colleagues and students helps to keep us honest and grounded as well as promotes a culture of transparency.

This next section outlines areas where people expressed opinions about areas of the program that could have been handled differently. There are four issues being outlined in the conversation. I would argue that the way in which people are able to speak so openly and honestly with each other speaks to the trust that was shared among the people participating in the conversation.

* * *

The first issue takes place between Peggy (an instructor) and Quisia (a counselor). Peggy worked at the Open Book from 1996 to 2001. She volunteered at the program for a year before she was hired. Quisia was hired at the Open Book in 1998, to replace Cecilia after she retired, and worked there until 2002. The issue that is being highlighted in the conversation is the possibility that staff meetings could have been conducted differently to engage or include more voices so that perhaps more people felt as if they had an entry point into the dialogue.

Peggy: We used to have staff meetings every Thursday afternoon and there was always a sense that students weren't allowed in those staff meetings. It always seemed like closed doors with no students allowed. I wonder why they couldn't be involved. In interviews where new people were hired, students participated in a fuller way in the management of the Open Book, but that was very infrequent. It happened only about once every two years. If students had come to those meetings, they would have been longer and maybe a bit more frustrating but more students would have developed more skills. Even with the assistant teachers, I was always struck at how they never said anything. They were so quiet. And I never suggested trying to work with Joan or Aida (the two assistant teachers). I know they met with John separately but that was different from the staff meetings.

Quisia: I think it would have been difficult to discuss issues with students there. I felt that sometimes, we the teachers had to discuss particular students and we needed a place to do it. I never felt power was in place there. We were always asked our opinions and when any particular situation that had to do with the school came up, John always threw it on the table for us to give our opinions. I agree, Joan and Aida were kind of quiet but I remember Aida sometimes expressing opinions. Joan was someone who was depressed.

Peggy: I agree that it would have been more uncomfortable to talk about certain topics with students there. And I think the meetings were great, I'm just questioning why we didn't try to involve students more. I think some students could have been developed even more than they did.

The second issue raised by Virginia and Cecilia also focuses on conducting staff meetings differently, in a more focused way.

Virginia: I've often thought that what was so great about something was sometimes also what was wrong with it. I remember sometimes disagreeing with John about meetings. I was always checking my watch thinking this is not going anywhere. I could sense that people were trying to feel out what John was thinking. What would John like to hear? But he was determined that it wasn't going to be about his agenda. He was not about to take charge! And sometimes I was more efficiency minded.... Let's get it done, somebody take charge here! I think sometimes the students would get angry too but ultimately he was right because speeding up would have destroyed the entire process. It felt excruciating sometimes but never boring. It was lengthy and messy but when the group got to a consensus, you could just feel when it's right.

Cecilia: I'm going to be honest with you. I hated the teachers' meetings. Sometimes they used to get into the methodic things about teaching and I thought people don't think that way. It wasn't real to me.

Virginia: Cecilia, you were our reality check.

Cecilia: I never really thought like a teacher.

Virginia: I remember once when John wasn't there, I was in charge of the meeting, and I decided this meeting was going to be about something. So I brought in materials about different ways of approaching reading comprehension. It was a different kind of meeting. Maybe one way to approach the problem would have been to let different teachers run the meetings. And I know that would have been welcome.

The third issue is raised by Nancy (an evening classes instructor), who taught in the program from 1986 to 1989. She raises the issue of whether more focus on teaching strategies at meetings would have supported her growth as a practitioner—in other words, some more focus on the "how to" instead of the "what for."

Nancy: In retrospect I think I would have benefited a lot from more discussions about actual teaching techniques. It was very challenging to run a classroom where people were at such a large range and although we struggled and John and I talked about it a lot, I would have benefited a lot from workshops. The strength of the Open Book was that it felt like such a humane place where we were just good human beings trying to do this type of work, but in the early years, we could have benefited from more strategies. I don't know if that would have involved more money. I know we hardly had any budget. I think it's very hard to go through the program when people work part-time and don't have the hours to plan, but this again is a money issue. It's certainly one of the reasons I moved on because I wanted more training and I also wanted to feel like I would have a more stable situation.

John: I think you're raising an important point. Having only part-time teachers was definitely a weakness. But that actually changed. Later on we were able to get people on staff benefits. Toward the end, four out of five teachers were on benefits. That last year, there were two people who didn't have benefits. Regarding the issue of techniques, I think there is a way that maybe the fact that we weren't rooted in a lot of different techniques opened up other possibilities. In my first couple of years, I really tried out a lot of things. I felt like in the beginning, I took more risks. There were some powerful people in the first class I taught. We were all having conversations about politics. I would write down the conversations, type them up, bring them back the next day, and we would read and write some more. I never do that anymore.

The final conversation takes place among Virginia, John, Cecilia, and Stacie (an evening instructor who worked from 1990 to 1994). The issue is centered on a student's writing involving the riots that took place in the Crown Heights section of Brooklyn in 1991. The incident leading up to the rioting was the death of a seven-year-old Guyanese boy, Gavin Cato, who was struck down by a vehicle driven by Orthodox Jews. Riots and lootings erupted rapidly in the area as long-simmering tensions between the black and Jewish communities boiled over. This anger led to a retaliatory killing of an Australian scholar, twenty-nine-year-old Yankel Rosenbaum, three blocks away from the Cato incident. The person accused of the killing was a sixteen-year-old African American, Limerick Nelson.

John: Stacie had a student in her class. A young woman from Haiti named Marie Caroline. I think she was only sixteen. She had been brought over here by her aunt, and she was forced to go to work, not allowed to go to school, sort of living like a slave. Anyway, with the riots in Crown Heights she wrote a story for the journal that was very hostile toward the Orthodox Jews in the community and Stacie really didn't feel like it should be printed. But it was a difficult dialogue and we had long conversations among the teachers about how to respond to the issue.

Stacie: We had long conversations with the students too.

Cecilia: I was really angry during this time because it was the first time, the only time, this girl really opened up. Before this she had never written anything. Her writing was poor but it was the one time when she was moved to write about something that happened in her community. She was very much against the Jewish community in Crown Heights because this Jewish man had killed a black boy. After she wrote it, they didn't put her piece in the book. And I knew that if her piece wasn't published, she would leave the class and I really didn't want her to leave. I thought talking to her might be a way to reach her and get her to open up.

John: I was actually in favor of publishing. In any case we decided to go back and talk to her about it some more. Ultimately she decided not to publish it. She withdrew the piece. It was really her decision. I think she recognized the teachers didn't really want to publish it the way it was. I guess she really didn't want to go up against the teachers, to be in that position. I'm not quite sure.

Virginia: I got the feeling that she started to realize the audience was bigger than our intimate space. I think that was what Stacie was thinking about too.

Cecilia: It was a very touchy situation but I think they should have talked to her and let her opinion stand because that's what she was feeling. It was the first time that she really wanted something of hers in the journal. Racist or not, it was part of her, what she was feeling. She shouldn't have been silenced.

John: That was exactly the question I think we were struggling with. A lot of what we were about was really creating space for voices that had been silenced. Yet here we were in a conversation about silencing and this actually relates to what we were trying not to do. We did actually talk with other students about this issue. However, I'm not sure whether they were really acceding because this is a teacher and whether left to their own they would have made the same choice. It's a challenging question. We discussed printing it and then saying this wasn't representative of how the program felt but we didn't feel right about that either. So, she ended up withdrawing the piece.

Cecilia: And that was letting the powers that be to be. That was how I saw it.

*   *   *

• The first issue that Peggy raised is the perceived exclusionary sense that could have been experienced by students regarding staff meetings. She questions why students weren't allowed. If the space truly belonged to everyone, then what invisible markers indicated the room was "off limits" during the time of meetings? Was it the closed doors? How did students really perceive those meetings? Was it perceived differently by different students? Was there the perception that the meetings were filled with inaccessible concepts and ideas? In other words, to what extent were we inadvertently reproducing a characteristic of the dominant culture? In what ways could sharing what was discussed at meetings been increased in order to foster more transparency with students? Would sharing always have been appropriate or helpful? Would it actually have contributed to the space being more democratic? (What about when specific students were being discussed?) Quisia's perspective on this is somewhat different. She believes power was not at play in this instance. But what if it were? To Foucault (1977) power is omnipresent, etched into the tiniest minutiae of our daily lives, into the deepest grains that define who we are. How then could we, as products of this dominant culture we live in, not bring some of that from the outside world into the Open Book? Would students' sense of agency have been promoted by attending staff meetings? Or would they have found them uninteresting? As students and practitioners, it is our responsibility to negotiate a new educational structure that does not reproduce the existing system (Johnson-Bailey, 2004).

• Peggy raises the issue of Aida and Joan (two of the assistant teachers) being reticent to speak at meetings. What were the reasons for this? Could they have felt uncomfortable because they were internally judging themselves by the dominant culture's standards of worthiness? To what extent would it have been possible to do otherwise? Did they feel they had to work harder for others in the room to listen to them and the prospect was too intimidating? Could it have been that in their separate meetings with John they covered the issues of importance to them and didn't perceive the larger meetings as being directly relevant to their interests and needs? Also, how did they view their roles at meetings? Was it more as listeners? What structures or supports would have needed to be in place to have changed their perceptions? These are complicated issues and dynamics but as literacy workers we need to be ever vigilant and attentive to them. Certainly in staff meetings, we need to find ways to support more people in entering conversations if it is to be truly inclusive. As Doyle (1993, cited in Brookfield, 1995) states, closing a door does not necessarily lock out students' social, cultural, political, or historical realities. Students' prior experiences may have produced legitimate fears, and those students may hold back, afraid their ideas may not meet with approval of others in the room (regardless of how inviting and welcoming some may perceive the space to be). As adult educators, it would be better to acknowledge publicly our position of power, to engage students in deconstructing that power, and to attempt to model a critical analysis of our own source of authority in front of them; doing so will sometimes involve us in becoming alert to, and publicly admitting, oppressive dimensions to practices we had thought were neutral or even benevolent (Brookfield, 2005).

• The second issue raised by Virginia is the meandering pace that meetings took on. She wonders how they could have been facilitated in more focused ways without sacrificing the process of critical analysis of issues that people felt were central to the program. In our society, we tend to focus on outcomes, solutions. Time is money, after all. However, often the type of collective questioning and analysis that allowed us to think and wade knee deep through thick swamps filled with murky issues and questions, prodding and probing our own and each other's consciousness, would not have been possible and may have been sabotaged in a neater, more efficient process, which Virginia does acknowledge. The model of taking charge is one we're all familiar with; it's perhaps less daunting to look for prepackaged answers from an external expert than turning that critical eye inward.

• Cecilia plainly states her frustration with teachers' meetings, saying they didn't reflect students' realities but teachers' perceptions of those realities. She thought the focus on methods "didn't feel real" to her. Could we as instructors have been unconsciously privileging certain ways of knowing above others? Namely, were we prioritizing the Eurocentric, rational models that the culture of schools promotes (almost everyone in the room had been successful in the school system, had done well at jumping through the hoops). Could people in the room have been inadvertently speaking to each other as "insiders" do, which left others who were less well served by the school system outside of the circle of educated doublespeak? Though in meetings we were able to challenge and probe each other's meanings, did we do so in ways that excluded or alienated certain members of our group? Virginia's suggestion of different people co-facilitating each meeting as a way of sharing leadership may have been one way of people's different contributions and ideas being heard and respected.

• Nancy's point about the limitations that part-time teachers present is as much of an issue in the adult literacy field today as it was when she was teaching at the Open Book. Most community-based organizations cannot afford to pay for full-time instructors. Having only part-time teachers definitely limits the possibilities of the program. Many part-time instructors piece together several jobs to barely make ends meet and are usually racing off to their next job after class. Usually in those programs, after classes end, the students leave also, often because there are no signs visible encouraging them to do otherwise. At the Open Book, I *was* hired on a part-time basis, which signaled the diminishing spaces that lay ahead for the program.

• In response to Nancy's comment about the possibility of more teaching techniques, I certainly agree that techniques can be very helpful to newer teachers. However, as John pointed out, not being wedded to techniques or ideas, operationalizing knowledge opened up space and possibilities to focus on vision. How we teach has a lot to do with how we expect and want people to be and what kinds of citizenship we encourage in learners (Nesbit, 2004). I agree that questions of method are secondary to those of paradigm. At the Open Book, our worldviews informed and guided us as we engaged in a collective journey of discovery. At other community-based organizations I'd worked in before the Open Book, there was a high volume of chatter on nifty, jazzy techniques but a disquieting lull in the conversation around what larger vision these techniques were rooted in—no connection of the critical nature of this work to larger political systems in this country.

• Last, John raises a complicated incident regarding a student's writing in Stacie's class. When space is made, are there unseen limitations, boundaries, or monitors on that space? In a program that strives to reflect students' voices to its very core, was there the perceived, gnawing, invisible sense of censorship? Of permitting visits to certain landscapes and strictly limiting others? Of silencing voices that had already been suppressed by mainstream culture? What are the dilemmas when this incident involves a student who hadn't shown much interest in writing yet was moved to write passionately about an act of injustice committed in her community? Then there are questions of the possible signals of disapproval sent to this student by staff. Were issues of positionality (the place where one is assigned based on membership in a group, with major categories being gender, race, class, sexual orientation, and age) at play (Johnson-Bailey, 2004)? Teachers were in positions of power after all. And what about when a student's words might hurt others and undermine the sense of community so many in the program were striving to promote? Whose role is it to protect that from being threatened, if it is? Other students apparently disapproved of the piece but as John questions, would there have been a different outcome to that discussion had instructors not been involved? Were students unconsciously seeking approval from the authority figure(s) in the room? Was democracy as a process being thwarted? By whom? As Heaney (personal communication, 2006) states, democracy is always exercised in the midst of struggle and conflict; democratic practice always exists in the face of contradictions both from without and from within. From without, it is confronted by layers of undemocratic practice. From within, by our inability or unwillingness to take responsibility for situations or understand the basis on which decisions are to be made.

What happens when democracy is so intimately intermingled with power, space, and voice and when most of us in society have never had any firsthand experience of what a democracy could look and feel like? What then would be some of the colors in a painting titled "Democracy"? How would the texture of the canvas feel? What would the paints smell like? How would it feel to make the first stroke with the brush on to the canvas? Who would make that stroke? The next chapter explores some of these questions.

EIGHT

Community Makes a Place Stronger!

The Issue of Power Revisited

The issue of power and its many threads spinning an iridescent web through the Open Book lies at the heart of this next conversation among Cecilia, Stacie, Nancy, John, and Virginia (all instructors in the program; John was the teacher-coordinator). They reflect on how their philosophies (both individually and collectively) impacted the program's culture. They also discuss the unique leadership style that contributed to the many openings and possibilities that occurred during the history of the program in terms of the ways teachers viewed their practice (and worked with each other) as well as the relationships they formed with students and the journeys they navigated and traveled together. Throughout the conversation, there was always an underlying question of whether the ripples of shared humanity and respect that flowed silently but persistently through the program were the result of a collective vision or one individual's (John's). The next conversation attempts to unpack some of the underlying dynamics grounded in power and its various patterns and swirls.

*   *   *

Stacie: I think I would have been happy if I had had a prewritten script to follow.

Virginia: There were so many extraordinary students and I think a lot of the strength came from them. Aida, for example, gave so much help to other students who didn't have the confidence.

Nancy: I actually feel like John gave a very strong spine to the program. What he did and what I loved actually was that he was my mentor in that he gave us permission to set up an alternative way of thinking. I felt because he was sort of our nominal head and because he, as organizing it, said to me, you can do it this way, [it] gave me the freedom to really concentrate on what was going to work for the students. You don't have to follow some kind of strict routine. You can be really flexible, thoughtful, and explore things. I think the vision he brought was unusual. In my experience, we don't get much of it in society actually. Everybody's usually very competitive, busy watching their back. You spend so much time worrying you're doing it wrong and somebody's going to tell you to do it differently. With John, I feel he set a certain tone and he did it very strongly, but the tone he set was very democratic. So he was a strong leader in the sense that he was protecting our space to allow us to find ways to be better with each other. I guess given the context of this society to have a program like this, you actually need some strong leadership. At least in setting it up, because you have to fight off the way the rest of society is. I think you need somebody with that confidence to say this is how we're going to treat each other.

Virginia: I thought of John as a leader. But you said it very well, Nancy. He gave us permission to do it right, to take it on ourselves, and to take responsibility to make it work.

Cecilia: To me John really was the spine, but you're forgetting something. The spine is not a steady thing; it is flexible. He was the spine because he was the center from which we all hung. He held on to everything but he wasn't a stiff spine. We had the flexibility to do things.

John: People would say, "Oh, it's John," but I don't believe that for a minute. I do think there's something to what you're saying, Nancy, and I'm much more comfortable with the way you're saying it. In a way, I created some space that allowed Aida, Yolanda, and everybody to make this ... place what it was and maybe I had some vision but I wasn't the one who made it. In a certain sense, I was only making some space. Everybody—the students, the teachers—then did something amazing with that space. I think it's really important that that gets understood.

Virginia: But the space had to be allowed because there's no model for that anywhere else.

John: Sometimes people had to fight for that space. It wasn't a done deal. There was always debate and expression over this issue.

Nancy: But even the way you handled that was to deal with it seriously and respectfully. To say, yes, it's good to have this. In other places I've been it felt like "you're wasting my time" or "I know better." That's why I would say the Open Book was about how community makes a place stronger!

Stacie: Yes, I think for me community is more than we are all in the same room working together. We actually have to be doing something else together in that room.

Nancy: What usually happens in other programs is when one person had more power, it usually meant the other person had less, but I didn't think that happened at the Open Book. It just seemed like when people got more power it was good because it meant it was shared.

John: It seems to me another way to think about this is that if we have some sort of process to come to agreement about something, then we're all made more powerful by that. It's not necessarily like a finite amount of control that we're all fighting for. My view has always been that the more power students had, the more powerful that made me in a way. So if I want to be part of a more loving, gentler society even if it reduces control over my decisions, it makes possible what is in my view a greater world, which is in my interest. So in which way am I more powerful? This issue of power to me is rooted in much more of a collective idea.

Virginia: I think community is like that. It just feels good if people strengthen. It makes everybody stronger.

Stacie: If you're thinking of power in terms of I walk into a classroom and I have already decided we're going to X and the students say no, we have no interest in studying that we want to study Y, my power isn't in choosing what we're going to study but in helping the students learn what it is they want to learn. It doesn't take away from me to have to give up whatever my lesson plan was. Instead, in this way, I am given something and they're given something.

Cecilia: I never really saw John's power. I remember in the beginning when he hired me he said we all have to be part of making a community so everyone has a voice. I always knew that he was not in the position of boss. The students were the boss; they're the ones who were going to benefit from this program.

Virginia: Yes, we became a community even though we all came from different backgrounds.

Nancy: Yes, I felt like I came from a very different background than most of the students. I had gone to an Ivy League school. I grew up in the suburbs. I guess I had a lot of education and some of my ideas were really different from a lot of the students'. But I remember when I had my daughter and I was trying to figure out how to manage teaching and be a new mother and one day Iris (a student at the Open Book) said to me, "Why don't you bring the baby to class? And put her in a corner?" It never occurred to me that I could do something like that and though I actually didn't do it, it just made me feel like we had really become a family together. You know, that I could ask things of the students too; it was okay to step over the line.

John: That description totally makes sense to me. At that time in the Open Book, there wasn't really that much being imposed from the outside. A lot of that intimacy, especially from the earlier years of the Open Book, slowly got eaten away by all of the formalities, the demands being imposed externally. I suppose part of that is looking at the values that really underlie this place, the structure of the place. What is the culture of the place? So in a way I saw it as an alternative to the dominant culture. I think the program was really a place that people could come and use for whatever they needed. I always felt that if we were in the South in 1964, the Open Book would have been a really different place. But we were in New York in this particular time so ... to what extent can a place like the Open Book support alternative ways of thinking? There was work around police brutality and welfare, which clearly made their way into the school, but the program couldn't really take on the role of being a general motor for changing society.

* * *

In the preceding conversation, we read some different strands of power being explored and each person's perception of John's leadership role, both as a space-maker and a protector of that space. Freire (1970) states that a

revolutionary leadership must practice co-intentional education. Teachers and students co-intent on reality, are both Subjects, not only in the task of unveiling that reality, and thereby coming to know it critically but in the task of re-creating that knowledge. As they attain this knowledge of reality through common reflection and action, they discover themselves as its permanent re-creators. In this way, the presence of the oppressed in the struggle for their liberation will be what it should be: not pseudo-participation, but committed involvement. (p. 69)

Auerbach (1991) adds that the best way for us to become professionals may be to act unprofessionally (according to dominant, mainstream definitions of professionalism): this means to work collectively, to challenge norms, by allying ourselves with students and resisting the kind of stratification that professionalism often implies. In essence, it means linking politics, pedagogy, and professionalism as different aspects of the same process.

• Nancy first comments on John giving permission (through subtle and not so subtle signals as well as those that were seen and unseen) to set up an alternative way of thinking, an alternative to the dominant culture that didn't thrive on competition and individuality but instead on nurturing and growing a set of shared understandings and collective meanings. It was almost as if each person who participated in the program were members holding up the rim of a gigantic, invisible, and very precious vessel. If one person grew tired, others helped her. Success wasn't determined by one shining star but instead was based on every person holding up the rim. People focused on nurturing each other, not on individualistic achievements or on outshining each other (and if someone came in with a model privileged by the dominant culture, it quickly became apparent that this model was not one that was recognized by the Open Book). Instead, the uniqueness promoted by the program was very different from what society privileges, which begins in schools with tests where people are sorted, classified, and differentiated by the examination, which functions as a normalizing gaze, surveillance designed to classify and punish (Foucault, 1977). The Open Book disrupted that assumption. Here, as Virginia points out, people were given the permission to do it right.

• As Nancy contends, John's leadership protected the space, allowing rare and beautiful plants to grow and blossom. She says he allowed us to find ways to be better with each other. Underwood (1994) notes that one of the problems in our society is that we think of schools as doing all the teaching, yet the most critical lessons are barely addressed. A much harder job to learn, she points out, is being human. We inhabit a society obsessed with coming up with the one correct answer, but we are not at all equipped to reside in a world of questions and uncertainty. Questions challenge and shake our thinking to its roots; they expand and deepen our ways of being in all its varying complexities. Learning to reside in a sometimes shadowy forest of inquiry and problem-posing was much more critical to us working at the Open Book than the "correct" answer.

• We once again reenter the conversation (though maybe from a different access point) regarding making space. John reiterates that while he may have created some space and even protected that space from harmful invaders wearing the disguise of administrators or funders, what people managed to grow in that space—the magical spaces they were able to visit and even possibly gain citizenship in, the sense of humanity rooted in a larger vision of society (and the world)—was not what John (or any other one individual) could have ever accomplished on his own. As Nancy eloquently states, community makes a place stronger! Underwood (1994) defines a community as a group of people who learn to live together in complex ways. At the Open Book, I believe this was the case.

• The issue of power is revisited and the top-down model, which is prevalent in society and much of the dominant culture, is critiqued. This model where knowledge and power are held by a minority and not disseminated or shared is what most of us are accustomed to (as evidenced by governments and families). Allman (1999) states that it's not just the poor who are alienated from decision-making, but the vast majority of people living in the world, regardless of their form of government. At the Open Book, there was a conscious decision not only to look different from most literacy programs but for us to collectively live out our vision. John outlines a different analysis of power, one in which the more power students have, the more powerful that made him. It is a power rooted in collectivity. As administrator, John was present at the site of the program more hours than most other staff and students, enabling him to shape the program in less visible ways. Even though he strove for transparency in decision-making, by virtue of his role and his positionality he undeniably had more influence than most people did. How hard did he have to work for others to listen to him? When he offered an opinion, to what extent did others automatically agree with him without probing the recesses of their own thinking (or even being conscious they were deferring to him)? In what ways was power camouflaged? Couldn't John ask students to leave the program, even though he didn't exercise that power? And again, though he didn't exercise this power, didn't he also have the power to hire and fire instructors? Or at the very least recommend someone be hired or dismissed? Issues surrounding power are not only complicated to unpack but are also fluid, ever changing depending on time, context, setting, and actors involved. Cecilia says, from the very beginning she perceived power as belonging to the students. After all, the program belonged to them. Did students also view it through those lenses? She also said she viewed John as the spine of the program. Can those two seemingly contradictory notions of power reside comfortably side by side? Were there students who might have perceived having considerably less power?

• Stacie speaks of power in her teaching as a process of supporting students in figuring out their goals, what they want their education and that process to look like, even if it contrasts with what she had originally planned for the class. In that way both she and they are given something; they are able to enter a relationship of mutuality and reciprocity.

• Nancy speaks of the trust and love that developed between her students and herself making them a family where they felt comfortable enough to ask things of each other, though they were from very different backgrounds. In education that is real and meaningful, one's heart and soul is transformed and there can never be a way back (Hart, 2001).

Yet the Open Book doesn't exist anymore. What happened? What went wrong? If it provided many with an experience permanently stamped deep into their consciousness, a space that changed so many lives, why wasn't it supported? Replicated? The next chapter unpacks some of the complexities behind the larger factors that ultimately led to the program being closed in 2001.

Nine

The Writing on the Wall

In the following chapter I outline and reflect on the events and underlying factors leading up to the closure of the Open Book. I could hear everyone's voices reverberating in my head, feel their hands gently guiding my pencil, standing behind me and looking over my shoulder as I wrote, see their eyes filled with silent tears as we all relived the loss of the program once again. I could hear the nuances in people's voices, what was being said as well as what was left unsaid, the unspoken words and the pain behind the pauses and the longer silences. I could sense the significance of people's words as they reflected on the transformation of their lives by and with this space. All of it would come rushing back to me, engulfing and drowning me in sadness and inconsolable grief. Now no one would ever experience the program, ever know the humane reality of the Open Book. Often during the night, the loss penetrated my dreams, piercing through my consciousness into my heart. When I woke up, for the first minute or two, I would experience unbearable sadness, my entire being filled with grief and loss. Then I would realize it was only a nightmare. But it wasn't just a nightmare (at least one from which I could awaken), and the sadness, the sense of loss, persisted. Perhaps the most wrenching pain came in thinking of the many students who would not succeed in other programs due to the policy restrictions placed on those programs. Yet at the Open Book everyone had always been welcome. Staff and students had made the decision that if the choice was being a shining star in the numbers game or working with students on bigger, process-oriented issues that took time (becoming a proficient reader would be one of those issues), then there really was no choice. It would always be the latter.

In the steady shifts in public funding policy for adult literacy, many programs can ask students to leave if they're absent more than a certain number of times. In order to continue receiving city funding, programs must maintain a certain number of people in the classroom. After the Open Book closed, I met former students who were asked to leave other programs in which they had enrolled. These students, who perhaps could initially be perceived as anxious, even angry, had led extremely difficult lives, who had suffered great losses. They were people who had countless reasons to feel rage and much more. Those same students found enough soil to flower and flourish at the Open Book in its enveloping atmosphere of acceptance and respect. They were perceived by the dominant culture as stunted, of less worth. However, at the Open Book we knew their bonsai status was a result of the restrictions forced on them by mainstream culture and ideologies. They knew they would be welcomed into the family for as long as they needed to be. Even today, other program directors in literacy programs still openly acknowledge the uniqueness of the philosophy of the Open Book and the commitment to work with all students, not just the easy ones. One former program director, who worked at the mayor's office of adult literacy, had this to say:

> In the eighties, there was enormous interest in the role of students' voice at the table and active participation. It was much more encouraged then. Now that's been totally marginalized but the Open Book was not only known for citywide efforts but John would be a resource, provide space for students to meet, would be there on Saturdays, might facilitate getting a proposal together, etc. There was something larger that was being embraced that no longer happens. The Open Book really shone in developing different student initiatives.

Another program director said, "There really was no program in NYC like the Open Book." Who then is serving this population that can arguably be considered the most vulnerable of an already marginalized segment of society? What are our commitments? Whom do we serve?

In the following conversation, Virginia, John, and Cecilia outline some of the reasons behind the Open Book becoming increasingly vulnerable to the changing tides as time went on.

*   *   *

Virginia: The lack of support from Good Shepherd Services was clear especially at the end as the agency leadership changed. I didn't

think we were defended at all. We were slowly being pushed. The
first sign was this ridiculous documentation of students. It became
all about the march toward that job. We were supposed to put
them on the scale and make sure they were on the next milestone.
How many hours did they work outside class? How much time did
they spend in class? It was such an invasion of their lives. This was
about the paperwork required for Good Shepherd funding sources,
documentation of everything. They wanted to see where people
started, what were the increments of their progress. I began to hate
it so much [because] it had nothing to do with the person; it was
just about little numbers. Good Shepherd wasn't interested in adult
programs. I'm not sure when they started changing their thinking
but they did. It felt like they started bothering us more and more
about the debt and the paperwork of the program. John started
getting more and more grief about student involvement and the
philosophy of the program. We started hearing more and more about
what was important according to the funders. They became more
and more reluctant to take over filling in the difference from the city
and state funding because sometimes these funds wouldn't show
up for half the year. The program would start the year and then get
refunded from the state and city and Good Shepherd became less
and less willing to do that.

John: The budget gave them power. Our funding didn't cover the budget.
We had budgeted $175,000 and we probably needed $250,000.
The typical program has some administration and a lot of part-
time teachers who are just paid for their class. The hourly rate is
approximately $70 an hour, so you pay that teacher $27 and then
basically you support the program through the gap between how
much you pay the teacher and how much you got per hour.

Earlier on, this was one of the struggles that I had with the
administration. So over time there're really two things happening.
There's pressure from the state and federal government and funders
in general to focus on core outcomes. At the same time there's the
way Good Shepherd reacts to that. Basically while I was there, they
built up a very big administrative structure. When I got there, there
was one person who paid the bills. They didn't even have a human
resource department. By the time I left, there's quality assurance,
development ... four or five people in fiscal and four people in
human resources. All of this is being paid for out of funding for
programs. They're all a kind of response to the demands from the

government, which focused on more accountability. That's part of the problem. I think a lot of people at the Open Book felt that the agency wasn't really committed to the program and therefore didn't really do the kind of fund-raising that they needed to do or make the kind of choices that people felt they should have made. The agency wasn't really committed to the Open Book. Their heart is in family and counseling services. Adult education is really low on their agenda. The program wasn't profitable for them. I think the program might have stayed alive another year or two if I hadn't left. I do think my leaving opened up the possibility for them. It would've been harder to force me out but they would have found a way to do it.

Virginia: They weren't honest with us about what their thinking was around these issues.

John: I think there were some other things in Good Shepherd that were really difficult and upsetting for us. One of them was in 1999. There was this Women and Literacy conference in Atlanta, and we really wanted Aida [an assistant teacher at the program] to be able to go. She was interested in going. The agency said they would pay for me to go because I was on staff but they wouldn't pay for Aida's expenses. For us this was such a tremendous opportunity. The reason they wouldn't pay was because she was only part-time. So we raised the money ourselves. We all contributed, it wasn't that much money because it was really just the plane fare. Aida went and I think it was a really powerful experience for her. But the agency came down on me. They said it was against policy to do fund-raising among the staff. It seemed like such a narrow rule that totally ignored the reality of what was going on.

Virginia: That was some of the handwriting on the wall. That was when I left. I had lost one of my jobs [within the agency] in the evening and it looked like I might lose the day one as well. I wasn't making enough money to support myself as it was so I started to look around. They weren't interested in any other way. The old Good Shepherd Services would have found another position for me easily but ...

John: This is somebody who gave an enormous amount of time to the agency.

Virginia: Almost twenty years.

John: This was just another indication that the agency was becoming corporatized, but the truth is I see this as more systemic than personal.

Cecilia: What makes me so angry is that for so long I worked without being paid. I did it because I love the Open Book and because I wanted to give something to the program.

Virginia: And whenever I think about that library ... all those books, all those pictures ...

John: They got rid of all of them.

Virginia: Those books were fantastic. I mean, there must have been somebody there who realized the value of that.

Cecilia: John, I think when they forced you to withdraw your writing from that publication, it was the last straw toward making you go. Before that you always had the freedom to write but not this time. But they [Good Shepherd] underestimated the strength of the program. Think about all the people that passed through the Open Book and benefited from it. They are going to pass on everything they learned there to their children, to their friends, who will pass it on to the people in their lives. In that way the program lives on. It's a continuing cycle ... that's the beauty of it.

Virginia: That's right. But forcing John to take his writing out of *Literacy Harvest* [a publication of literacy practitioners' writing] was pretty awful.

John: I think that was definitely a factor in my leaving but really it had mostly to do with what the place had become. It became somewhere I felt less and less comfortable in. Cecilia's right, though; after the incident with the article, I made the decision to leave. You know, I feel like we live in a society that dehumanizes people so tremendously. The culture and values that people are bombarded with day after day.... I saw the Open Book as an effort to create an environment that was in some ways an alternative to that.... The field is a creation of the government. How can it be about social change?

*   *   *

In the conversation above, Virginia, John, and Cecilia talk about the dwindling agency support that led to the closing of the Open Book and outline some factors defined by the external, increasingly gloomy political landscape and shifting priorities of the Good Shepherd Services administration.

• Virginia refers to the lack of support being especially clear with the switch of adult education directors (within Good Shepherd Services). This change occurred in 1996. Prior to that, John's supervisor, the director of community-based programs, had been someone who was perceived by the staff as being more supportive of the Open Book's philosophy, which was rooted in a participatory vision of education. Virginia also mentions the documentation and other ominous signs of bureaucratization where people were increasingly being viewed as statistics to maintain funding and ensure the program's survival. In the political climate in which adult literacy programs operate in New York City, if a program refuses to comply, what are the ramifications? Is it a realistic option to even consider resisting the onslaught of the current tide? There's the increasing perception that the agency wasn't fully committed to the program. Instead, funders' mandates were the only drivers of a train moving at lightning speed, students were barely hanging on from the outside, with both arms locked in what could be considered a deadly embrace or fervent prayer. The train was gaining speed with every turn until at the very end the only people who stayed on did so at their own risk. As Virginia says, the aspects of education that were considered important were being determined by funders.

• John speaks of the burgeoning administrative structure, which the program budget was being used to partially support. What restrictions was the program forced to shoulder as a result? It was apparent in the preceding conversation that people acutely felt the lack of commitment. It also became clear that the funders were behind the wheel and that students were in the backseat (if not the trunk). What were the effects, both seen and unseen, of having that shadow cast over everyday operations at the program? The role of an umbrella agency is usually to protect, not steadily chip away at one of its programs. Did Good Shepherd have a choice but to toe the line regarding policy or was there another less defined path it could have chosen? John asks, if the field is essentially created by the government, through funding and the requirements to maintain that funding, then how can social change be fully realized when that's not in the primary interest of funders?

• John recounts the incident involving Aida (an assistant teacher) wanting to attend the annual Women and Literacy conference in Atlanta, Georgia, but the agency would not pay her expenses because she was a part-time employee. Aida, in an earlier conversation recalling her experience of attending the conference, had the following to say: "Attending the conference was great. It made me feel like I wasn't alone. I realized there were other people out there going through similar experiences to me. It was really good for me to attend. I really enjoyed it." Yet the agency would not budge an inch regarding the program's request that Aida attend. From the very beginning, the Open Book perceived much of its work as defined by supporting students' rights yet the agency couldn't seem to follow suit. As Virginia said, in many ways the writing was on the wall: a signifier of a sinking ship already collecting water.

• Virginia refers to the old and new Good Shepherd Services, implying the sets of possibilities would certainly have been different under the old Good Shepherd. The new Good Shepherd is driven by the larger sociopolitical context of shifting priorities—the swinging of the pendulum that evoked a sense of foreboding and dread from literacy workers—intimately connected to the issue of the agency's corporatization. Essentially, staff at the program perceived how the impact of the work they were engaged in with students gradually began to be viewed in terms of economic currency. It was being measured in terms of dollars and cents instead of by looking at more qualitative aspects involving, for example, a group of students standing around a coffee machine during the class break chatting about their lives and struggles, exchanging advice and offering support, engaging each other in ways no testing instrument can easily quantify, except that these ways continue to live deep in people's consciousness. By living and participating in this world, the students and staff from the Open Book continue to impact others in daily interactions. As Cecilia mentions, in that sense, the program continues to reside in all of us who participated in it. The impact isn't measurable but is real, definite, and powerful in infinite, intangible ways that defiantly refuse to be quantified!

• There was an enviable library at the Open Book. It was an airy room flooded with sunlight, a small round table in one corner with chairs around it and a sofa against an adjoining wall. But upon entering, one's eyes couldn't help but be drawn to the bookshelves that lined the walls, filled with hundreds of books in seemingly countless categories and varying levels of difficulty. Many students made those books their own and the characters their personal friends, as they encouraged other friends to read books they loved. It was a magic moment to overhear one of those conversations filled with passion and engagement as students stood around, impervious to anyone else, arguing details of the plot, the attributes or lack thereof of characters, and other reactions to the text. Somehow they had met in the spaces that existed among letters, words, and sentences on pages and learned ways of dancing out shared meanings together. All of those books were discarded by Good Shepherd Services. It was a staggering loss to those of us who worked in the program and had witnessed as well as participated in the spaces/places that were accessed from that room ... a tunnel into magical worlds where every page and conversation offered the opportunity to stand on the brink of a cliff, a revelation, where with just one small step you could soar weightlessly through entire other universes of possibilities.

• Then there is the issue of the article John wrote for *Literacy Harvest* entitled "Zigs and Zags: Doing Literacy in the Era of the WIA." After John wrote the article, he was told to withdraw it because he hadn't followed procedure. He was told he should have submitted it to the agency first for approval. Even though it was unsaid, few were fooled into believing content wasn't an issue. If the article hadn't been critical of adult literacy public policy, would the result have been different? (To read the complete article, see Appendix E.) Earlier, in 1995, John had been asked to write another article (see Chapter 6 for an excerpt), yet the winds had now changed direction. This was a strong sign that the pockets of democracy had diminished. The borders for resistance had been clearly drawn and anyone who stepped over paid dearly. But where was the line? What if you couldn't see it? Good Shepherd was responding to the larger political direction in New York City during this time. Yes, they probably could have been more supportive, many different scenarios could have played out, but what are the chances of survival for the Open Book and other programs like it in the bleak, arid desert that the field is forced to operate in, where no protection from the harsh, howling elements is offered, and where gentler forms of life stand a great risk of being destroyed or are forced to adapt into something harsher and scalier? This toxic whirlwind defined as policy must change if different forms of life are to grow and find nourishment.

• John says that after the incident involving his article, he made the decision to leave. How could someone who was a part of a program defined by recognizing students' basic rights to dignity and democracy, making space for voices and perspectives to be heard, live with censorship and not acutely be aware of the long-reaching implications underlying the request of being asked not to submit this article? How could the price of staying committed to the principles and philosophies of the Open Book be quantified?

• As people point out again and again in the preceding conversation, the Open Book wasn't just about teaching reading and writing in a different way. It offered instead a vision of what could exist, a different way of being. It spoke to a larger way people could learn to live with each other. As Freire (1970) points out, we cannot consider ourselves to be in a state of well-being when segments of our community are suffering. Freire and Macedo (1987) go on to reiterate that the new literacy programs must be largely based on the notion of emancipatory literacy, in which literacy is viewed as one of the major vehicles by which oppressed people are able to participate in the sociohistorical transformation of their society (p. 157). Is the mainstream society ready and prepared for this? From evidence around us, the answer seems, clearly not. But, what would it take for society to learn to be ready? Ornelas (1997) adds that in maintaining a relationship with the community, all actions are political. "We cannot be naïve about this. The two choices are to be functional and give charitable assistance, or be transformational. You are either with the people or against the people. There is no middle fence to sit on. With a charitable approach, nothing essential will happen. What is our choice? Aspirin or transformation?" (p. 170). The Open Book was a place where I (and as evidenced through the preceding conversations, many others) understood deeply and maybe for the first time what an honor and privilege it was to hold such a beautiful possibility of a different world in our hearts and labor together toward seeing it become a reality.

If we had a map of possible routes to take from this moment, what would it look like? The next chapter offers an update from the field, focusing on the progressively worsening condition and shrinking spaces in which literacy programs continue to struggle to survive in. Chapter 10 also issues a call to action to the adult literacy community.

TEN

Where's East? Where's West?

An Update from the Field

As a literacy worker, I serve in a field that is fraught with contradictions, struggles, and disconnects, but regardless, it continues to be a field I feel privileged and honored to be a member of. Over the years, I have witnessed the disheartening, steady shift of priorities and have seen adult literacy programs squeezed by deflating public funding. The Open Book and other adult literacy programs were funded under the New York City Adult Literacy Initiative (NYCALI), an initiative that coordinated the use of federal, state, and city funds into one system. Under this initiative, federal regulations required programs to report gains made by students in order to maintain funding. The primary outcomes recognized by this system are educational gain on standardized tests and those related to employment. In other words, did programs help that student find and maintain a job? Did learners score higher on standardized tests? In New York State, adult basic education programs are mandated to use the Test of Adult Basic Education (TABE), which as Virginia points out below, is inappropriate for capturing literacy progress (specifically reading) in any meaningful way.

Virginia recalls an incident with a student from the Open Book who was inadvertently given the wrong level of the TABE when the program switched to the new version of the test.

Virginia: Edami took the reading test. She first took the level E [Easy] and she scored a 4 [which was equivalent to a fourth-grade reading level]. Then she took the M [Moderate] and got a 6 [sixth-grade reading level]. Finally she took the D [Difficult] and got an 8 [eighth-grade reading level], which was more or less her real level. It was just insanity because you couldn't really use these things as markers ...

It is insanity that these tests are used as an indicator to mark progress while paying little or no attention to the following questions. Is the student reading whole texts? Is she actively engaged in the process? Can she talk meaningfully about what she read? Is she able to make inter- and intra-textual connections? Are there vital conversations going on around books in and out of the classrooms at programs (Calkins, 2000)? These are much more accurate indicators as to whether a student is on his way to becoming a more proficient reader. It can probably provide some indicator or insight into that student's test-taking skills but certainly doesn't provide any insight into his literacy proficiency. Short decontextualized passages don't measure literacy abilities (especially if the text involves themes that are either unfamiliar or of low interest to the reader) and are actually in direct opposition to cognitive strategies proficient readers use during the reading process (Kucer, 2001). However, today in most adult literacy classrooms, few or none of those questions count. Inevitably, in many literacy programs in New York City, there is now a strong focus on improving test-taking skills. Instruction consists more and more of workbook-type activities because those mimic what students are most likely to encounter on the TABE, and if they show high gains on this instrument, the program is considered exemplary by funders. Slowly but steadily, a culture of K–12 schooling is being replicated around the literacy community (Macedo, 1994). Funding certainly supports it. The system, by disempowering teachers and students, is then able to maintain itself in a sure and secure way by the direction of the field; threats to the status quo are steadily squashed. There is little support in current adult literacy policy that encourages programs to explore new ways of teaching and learning, to engage in practitioner research, and to adopt a stance rooted in inquiry.

The current climate is one of individualism and shrinking resources regarding adult literacy funding. Where are the spaces to engage in what John, Virginia, and Peggy speak about, which occurred on a regular and continuous basis at the Open Book?

John: From very early on we put an emphasis on collaboration. As teachers, we met a lot more than most programs and we talked things over among ourselves and with students. One thing we did well as teachers at the Open Book was read things together and try them out. I remember once, we read an article, "Teaching as Research," by Eleanor Duckworth, who teaches at Harvard in the graduate school of education. She's someone who tries to get teachers to think about how people learn, how to experience learning. So she had her students observe the moon and keep a journal of their observations. Every day she had them watch the moon and write down what they observed. We decided to try it out in class. Most of us who grew up in the city know nothing about the moon. So, I brought these little pads to class and asked everybody to go home and watch the moon and write down whatever they liked ... and we talked about the moon. Where's East? Where's West?

Virginia: I loved those school projects. Do you remember Street Law? The whole school really loved doing that.

Peggy: Yes, Nicholas, the evening teacher, started that. It was a sort of radical crash course for people in how to deal with the law, what your rights were and how you should deal with the police if they harass you. I learned so much and I remember thinking at the time that this was an area where teachers could learn so much from students because generally speaking, students have a lot more experience with the legal system.

John: The way Street Law developed was pretty interesting. We had asked a friend of mine who was a Legal Aid lawyer to come and speak to the class. While he was speaking, one of the students asked him how he liked being a lawyer and Bob (my friend) said that he loved being a lawyer because it gave him a socially useful way to deal with his anger. Nicolas later told me that as Bob was saying that, a light went on in his head, and at that moment he decided to become a lawyer.

Virginia: I saw him recently and he's a lawyer. He even told me it was Street Law that inspired him to pursue becoming a lawyer.

Cecilia: You know, I never remembered taking much from the outside. I remember listening to the students and giving them the opportunity to develop their own desire to take part in their own education. I remember one of the first things John gave to students was a cartoon with a person's head opened up and someone else trying to put something into their brain. He said students shouldn't be like that. The teacher is not supposed to be putting things inside the students' heads. That is not the way to learn.

John: That's the gasoline pump cartoon from a book called *Training for Transformation.*

Cecilia: I remember being so touched by you not wanting to push things onto the students.

Virginia: Every year we made it a point as teachers to talk about how we wanted to approach things differently. Sometimes it was talking about different readings because every year we always read texts with students that allowed them to talk about their previous history with education. It was often how we started the year. We wanted students to think about a different way to approach education where they could take charge.

Again, what elements need to be present in order to engage in and explore some of what Virginia, Cecilia, John, and Peggy discuss in the conversation outlined above? In 2011, many programs could hardly afford to pay their part-time instructors to attend *any* staff meetings, never mind staff meetings that focus on thick, rich conversations like the ones we had at the Open Book, conversations that left you drunk with possibility. At the Open Book, instructors immersed themselves in talk that was grounded in collectively growing as practitioners, reading articles that seamlessly blended theory and practice and then critically discussing them, and being completely committed to ultimately serving students in deeply meaningful ways that grow democracy. There was an inquiry-based stance where questions were asked on top of other questions, where people recognized that they learned by doing, as John pointed out in the unit on studying the moon and students writing down their observations, or Street Law where students learned about their rights and law enforcement. Though I didn't realize it at the time I was working there, we were engaged in a pedagogy of questioning, resisting, and contesting sacred truths regarding mainstream literacy. We had become a space that was intent on transforming both the world and the word (Torres and Fischman, 1994).

Currently, program directors are being forced to spend so much of their time struggling to keep up with the onerous and mounting pile of bureaucratic requirements in order to maintain funding—filling out forms, testing students more often, documenting goals (primarily employment), and following up with those goals (primarily employment)—there is no time left to struggle and grapple with the terrain we engaged in at the Open Book. The system is splintered, and we in the field are burdened with increasing demands. Programs have become so preoccupied with testing and performance measures, little time is left to focus on education, and even less for conversation that could threaten the status quo. Talk, after all, is dangerous. There is no time to hold town hall meetings, to talk with students and really get to know them, to publish student writing in serious ways, or to do the work with students around supporting and growing student leadership and building a democratic community. Certainly, this doesn't seem to be how NYCALI was originally envisioned.

The Story of NYCALI

The story of the New York City Adult Literacy Initiative is rooted in the serious financial crisis of the 1970s. The state had taken over the management of the city's finances and sold bonds to bail it out. In the 1980s those bonds matured and the city had all of these new monies. Mayor Koch, as a result of a report on dropouts in New York City and as part of his economic development plan, put $35 million into adult literacy. With this infusion of funds, NYCALI was born and the Open Book and thirty-five other community-based adult literacy programs and other programs throughout the city were funded. This initiative was a combination of federal (Workforce Investment Act—Title 2), state, and city funding. In the following conversation, Vincent, an individual with a long history in the field of adult education, reflects on some of the foundations that were laid in order to make NYCALI possible but also how this initiative changed from how it was originally envisioned to a tool for gatekeepers in the field to use to promote accountability.

Vincent: While the funding for NYCALI began in 1984, the work to design the initiative and get the political support happened several years before. What evolved into the current NYCALI was really from President Johnson's anti-poverty legislation from the 1960s. At that time the only federally (Adult Education Act) funded agency in New York City was the Board of Education and the only way you could offer classes (in that system) was to have their teachers come to your center, and so that's what we did. But it was all according to their curriculum, their time frame, and their holidays. I mean it was really "take it or leave it."

But we were having so many problems with the Board of Ed. so we formed a coalition called the Coalition for Adult Education Providers that was really a self-appointed advisory council for the Board of Ed. They didn't organize us; we organized ourselves. We started letting State Education know this made no sense! Funding needed to be opened up. A lot of the groups themselves had strong political connections that the legislature wanted to be responsive to. When the state finally opened up funding so that community-based organizations could access it, it was just a major, major coup.

Anyway, there was a report that was done on youth dropouts. The researcher, who later moved to the mayor's office, and was the major force in the creation of NYCALI, began asking why these young people were dropping out of school. What was happening to them? Are they going to get back into education? If so, where were they going? She then began interviewing all of us adult education providers because we were working with those students who did make it back into the system. So here's this report on dropouts and here we are trying to get direct and expanded funding for adult education. We had already worked to get the state to open up its funding, and then we worked with them on developing ways of reporting. We even did some hearings in Albany and here in the city for politicians on the needs of adult learners and its impact on the workforce.... Literacy was seen as part of economic development. Since we had been working with them about legislative issues, they would come to the hearings and become very involved. We thought, "Why don't we do this together?" The city agreed and the state agreed and that's how NYCALI was born. But it did feel like there was more space for progressive dialogue. The first NYCALI proposal included expectations of class sizes, curriculum, and staffing that were all rooted in progressive philosophies. However, at that time there was only federal money. It just felt great to be able to institutionalize all the coalition work that we'd done for years. We wanted NYCALI to have a strong research component because so much of it really grew out of the community experience and the mission of social justice. In the 1980s the struggles were more about building capacity that was high quality. In the earlier period of NYCALI, we looked at all the key elements, not just the federal accountability measures. We asked: do we have the voices of learners? Are we collaborating across city agencies in ways that are making the best use of the resources? Can we strategically expand the resources that are available in equitable ways?

We invited people to help us look at this. Researchers like Hannah Fingeret, Steve Reder, Hal Beder, Tom Sticht. We were constantly asking people, "What do you think?" That's much less the case now. The government's broader agenda (being the main funder) sets the agenda in New York in many ways. Before, funders and practitioners would talk about how we could make learning relevant to students' lives. How can that learning be transformational? How does it impact the community in ways that create more equity? Now that has changed. With only part-time teachers, the field is weak. Short-term funding changes constantly, legislative priorities change, amounts of funding change, and programs are chronically underfunded. The implications of these shifting priorities are enormous. The students certainly are marginalized; the practitioners are also marginalized, even though they may have been in the field their whole lives. There's the impact of what the public's willing to spend money on, how adult learners want to invest their time, the demands and changes in the school system, and what that means to parents in terms of the support they need to give their children.

Data collection has come more to be seen as an accountability measure as opposed to informing policy and developing quality practices. The students' voice at the table and active participation has been totally lost or marginalized. Now there really is no organized access to funders. Welfare reform also shifted things enormously. Literacy programs were forced to shift their focus from education to employment. Be on time, listen to your boss, and respect authority (as opposed to a model of empowerment, of community development, of change). Popular education, as practiced at the Open Book, without sufficient funding will be marginalized forever. For sure, there is a gap right now. All of the programs' work gets translated into a report card with just four outcomes on it and only one of them has to do with education. None of them have anything to do with the content or purpose of education. Because these report cards may jeopardize funding, they end up driving the discussion, the energy, and what few resources are available. We need to continue to push for more meaningful information that really expands the dialogue—otherwise we're left with no ammunition to support the education work that we do and counter welfare reform, immigration policy, and national security priorities. All of these things radically impact how adult education feels nationally. The changes of politics in our state reinforce this, and combined with the ongoing marginalization of the field through inadequate funding and a part-time workforce, the field is disabled from even advocating. Basically what's left are individuals who are very much on the margins.

We learn through Vincent's words that the emphasis and intent is on policing and gatekeeping instead of exploring how strong practice and philosophies could be linked to community development. Quality cannot be forced but instead must be gently nurtured and grown. Vincent says the goals of the original NYCALI were grounded in fostering equity, conducting research, working toward including more voices in decision-making, and developing a sense of agency within communities. The 1980s was a moment in time in the adult literacy community that was grounded in openness and inquiry. Policy, as Vincent notes, was much more supportive and aligned with the spirit and central tenets rooted in the Open Book. He also states that literacy policy was driven and shaped by factors around the country. Because the literacy world is located within a political context, for better or worse, it is impacted by larger events and political whims. One example is welfare policy. (See Chapter 6 for more on this.) These shifts in policy are recognized by a significant number of literacy workers as detrimental to our field but they occur regardless, swung into motion by the tentacles of capitalism. Programs are measured by outcomes, yet only one outcome has anything to do with education. Whose purpose is being served by keeping these formulas intact?

Literacy programs are being sent a resoundingly clear message that the overriding element in this formula is numbers. Each day, students and practitioners in the field are being alerted as to how unstable and precarious the situation in New York is for adult literacy programs. By permanently operating with insufficient funds, the focus shifts to survival instead of a collective dialogue envisioning something better: something that reminds us of the possibility between freedom and imagination—the ability to make present what is absent, to summon up a condition that is not yet (Greene, personal communication, 2005). In the numbers game, everyone competes for the same insufficient pot of funding. Keeping interests divided ensures people are not working together in strategic ways to effect change. Numbers are being used inappropriately to maintain a system whose interest is in maintaining itself (Peterson, personal communication, 2006). As Vincent points out, nowhere in this is there room to grapple with issues surrounding student involvement in decision-making—developing curricula built on themes and concerns articulated by students, growing a sense of community, attempting to place students at the heart of everything that's done in the program, and exploring what that could look like—as was attempted at the Open Book.

Instead, there is almost a paralytic sense that these rules are seemingly set in stone. People in the field accept this reality as unchangeable partially because there are few alternatives being laid out as viable options. Committed leaders who fought for spaces for and with students are now just fighting to keep their own programs alive. The energy and activism that were so ingrained in the field in 1990 seem difficult to sustain in the face of unsupportive legislation and hostile policy. Vincent raises the issue of how weak the field is at the moment; basically people are very much on the margins. I am equally disturbed that many people who are now joining this field seem to have internalized these new definitions of literacy: getting a job and making educational gains on standardized tests. As Morrow and Torres (1995) say, this struggle of attempting to overcome oppression, discrimination, and the deep structuring of subjectivities with classist and racist overtones has had a long history and many anonymous heroes. Although this isn't the time to romanticize the struggle, neither is it a time to nurture historical amnesia. Blaming communities for certain things is what the dominant culture does well; however, it refuses to see or deliberately won't see how much less those communities are given to begin with.

What lies ahead? Is it bypassing federally funded programs? Regardless of the fact that these programs have a responsibility to protect their citizens and that those citizens have a basic right to education? I believe it is critical for these issues to be viewed as a part of a larger picture. The literacy field is in a state of emergency. And it is essential for everyone (students and nonstudents) to think about how limited resources are going to be shared more equitably. Who will have access to and control these resources? How will they be disseminated?

Operating in a purely individual way doesn't serve anyone's interests, yet why do we cling to and police systems that clearly divide us, which makes us vulnerable as a field? We glory in the fact when we're given more funding even if it's at the cost of another program being defunded, displacing other students. Students must be supported so that the voice at the policy table representing their interests will be their own (Sparks and Peterson, 2000). One of the more insidious elements in this is that many policy-makers have never spent any time in classrooms or talking with students, so the stereotype of adult literacy students as not "getting it" the first time around, of bodies without promise, remains unchallenged. The blame continues to lie firmly with students instead of the deeply entrenched barriers and institutionalized *isms* (racism and sexism to name just two) that are blocking the way of those outside the dominant culture. The hundreds of thousands of poor people of color are seen as a ticket to reducing the cost of labor (Dyson, 2007). I have talked with many adult literacy students who point to the fact that even after they get a job, they earn practically slave wages. The business community is firmly in the driver's seat.

As a field we must organize in strategic ways that don't alienate but bring communities and different groups together. Literacy workers who feel that policy must be drastically changed to include students' voices and reflect their interests must come together with students—and not only in times of crisis. There needs to be a recognition that our coming together must be grounded in sustainable partnerships that recognize that what benefits one of us must benefit all of us. We must find ways to be more visible. How can we begin and sustain dialogues as a field? How and to whom will we tell our stories in all their richness and complexities? What must we do to stop the tail wagging the dog when the tail is the business community or politicians? How can we ensure politicians take the next step and follow up supportive talk with real action? In what ways can we resist the dominant frames or at the very least insert our voices and by doing so impact them? How can we rid ourselves of these shackles that seek to oppress, imprison, and exploit and collectively ensure these systems are made transparent, working together toward the dismantlement of such toxicity? How can we subvert the systems that claim to have an interest in working to eradicate illiteracy but keep intact such horrific economic inequity? How can we ensure that certain communities aren't targeted? Using inconsequential sums of money for programs that attack only the symptoms but keep alive this modern-day caste system in which we live isn't an option. The questions swirl and swirl in my consciousness, raising and forming new ones. I don't pretend to know the answers to all of these questions. But I believe these questions must be raised. The answers instead need to come from the field as we move forward together with new mandates, new questions, a new dream.

Soul Poem
Class Poem (1998)

My soul
moves like loving wind
feels like it wants to run and fly
looks like a beautiful sea
My soul
has been seen around the world
and dreams about being free

In the next and final chapter, I reflect on the process and journey (both personal and collective) as well as look ahead to the future of the literacy community. I also unpack personal implications, implications for the field, and implications that transcend the field.

ELEVEN

It May Be Finished but It Still Lives On!

The Plum Tree
Bertolt Brecht

In the courtyard stands a plum tree,
The little tree can't grow,
It wants to grow!
but it gets too little sun.
No one believes it's a plum tree
Because it doesn't have a single plum.
But it is a plum tree;
You can tell by its leaves.
(Brecht, 1938, p. 243)

According to the 2003 National Assessment of Adult Literacy Survey, 93 million in the United States have either basic or below basic level in prose or quantitative literacy. In New York City, according to data released from the mayor's office of adult literacy, over 2 million adults need adult education services but there are fewer than 60,000 seats available. Today in America and much of the world, books may be available but the politics of literacy and gatekeeping—who decides who reads, what they read, and for what purpose—is still very much maintained and perpetuated (Aronowitz and Giroux, 1985; Shor, 1987). Worpole (1977) adds that history has clearly shown that when the purposes of literacy are considered too radical and threaten the status quo, active measures are taken to marginalize or abolish that threat (p. 190). Literacy education in this country and elsewhere in the world is still very much entrenched in issues rooted in access, politics, and power (Freire, 1970; Purcell-Gates and Waterman, 2000). In the classless, individualistic society we live in, where the myth of the level playing field thrives, where people are expected to pull themselves up by their own boot-straps (a physically impossible task), space to address social inequalities, structures of domination, and multiple oppressions is obliterated (Luttrell, 1997; Macedo, 1994; Martin, 2001).

In adult literacy education, participants' stories chronicling the history of the Open Book highlight a different model, one that acknowledged class differences, racism, and larger structural inequities that directly impacted students' lives and often crippled the communities in which they lived. From the program's inception, people's accounts point to an alternative vision, where collectively people could co-create new visions of what could be, as well as acknowledge the pockets of hope that already exist (Fine, 1996). As evidenced by people's stories, at its core was a program that strove to fashion its existence and relevance around needs that emerged from the community of South Brooklyn where it was housed. Part of the contradiction and dilemma that clearly emerged from the story is that the interests of the field didn't and don't reflect the interests of the government (many would argue they are in direct opposition). As John points out,

> Many of us came into adult education because we believed in the transforma-
> tive power of adult education. We believed learning to read and write had
> the potential to give students the skills to understand and act on their world
> more effectively ... to act in concert with others to change the conditions
> of life in their communities ... but literacy funding is primarily aimed not
> so much at education but at re-education, not so much at giving people the
> academic and intellectual tools they need to better control their destiny ...
> but rather to convince them that they have no choice ... no matter how bad.

We learned that from the beginning at the Open Book, simultaneous co-teaching and co-learning occurred. Students related their own struggles to other students; students were hired as assistant teachers, which institution-alizes the notion that students have valuable things to teach both students and nonstudents. By students forming and participating in committees, participating in and facilitating town hall meetings, or by space being cre-ated for students to participate in all levels of decision-making affecting the program, growing a more democratic environment was being supported. An inclusive dialogue around decision-making developed, ranging from what books would be read in class to themes that emerged as units of study for instruction (see Chapter 3). Somehow an invitation was being issued, one aimed at a second chance, a different conclusion. We learned through people's words that community and the power of the collective were two honored cornerstones of the Open Book. We also learned through students' stories of painful scars etched deep in their consciousness inflicted by their prior school experience, judged by the dominant culture for not successfully fulfilling the demands of a system that didn't have their best interests at heart. Stuckey (1991) points out that literacy education begins in ideas of the socially and economically dominant class, taking the form of socially acceptable modes. Becoming literate therefore signifies in large part the ability to conform. When students fall outside of the mainstream categories, they are at an instant disadvantage regarding the value-laden culture of schooling (Heath, 1983). Hazel's, Antonia's, and Edami's stories show us how embedded these scars are and how great the cost is of our educational system to entire communities.

The very act of returning to school required remarkable courage on the part of these women. As Hazel said, "This was my last try; if I didn't make it here, that was it. I wasn't going to make it ever." For many students, returning to a space fraught with pain and struggle signifies a desire and quest to gain visibility, voice, autonomy, and respect. This effort shouldn't in any way be minimized or trivialized. For so very many, adult literacy programs represent a last glimmer of hope in education, in redefining what's possible in their lives, and also what's possible for us as a society. How will we be judged in the future and by whom?

People's stories also repeatedly point to the various ways they were marginalized in school or other literacy programs. I would urge peers, colleagues, and policy-makers in and beyond the literacy field to listen to that. In my view, among the most important elements of any literacy program is honoring and supporting students' basic right to "become somebody" (Luttrell, 1997). Adult education represents as much as anything else an opportunity and a quest to redefine an identity that's been imposed by dominant ideologies. An adult literacy program can become a site for students to become actors in a script in which they can rewrite their lives.

Earle: I would like to encourage teachers and directors in literacy programs to listen to students. It is very important to listen to what they say and allow them to be innovative, to be themselves, to grow as people, to be an entity, to be part of something that could be great.... Let students drive the vehicle.

Antonia: We come to these programs because something in our lives didn't go right. Something didn't happen in school for us and we need encouragement. We need to hear, "You can do this"; we need to hear, "It doesn't matter what level you are, you can bring yourself higher." ... We need someone to say, "You're not just another number passing through here; you're a human being and you came here with so many struggles and dreams."

People described feeling like "somebody" at the Open Book. Both to themselves and to others, they're remaking themselves. In my view, it is imperative for adult education programs to provide space for this to happen. At the Open Book, some of this happened through student committees (see Chapter 5), through students being hired as assistant teachers (see Chapter 4), through town hall meetings where students were asked their opinions and could then witness those opinions impacting ways the program was shaped, through writing and having their work read and honored by other students (see Chapters 2 and 3), by seeing issues and concerns from their lives treated seriously and by instructors developing units of study around these themes. Instructors were co-learners with students, practicing principles of democracy in all its tensions and contradictions (see Chapters 5, 7, and 8). Luttrell (1997) says, "adult education is about establishing a credible, worthy self and public identity as much as getting a diploma" (p. 126). People's lives, their interests and concerns, their selves should be at the center of programs.

Within literacy programs, I would recommend writing and publishing as one way to support this journey. Writing can be a potentially powerful opportunity for students to discover their own voice and clarify their feelings about issues that can lead to scrutinizing systemic inequities (see Chapter 3 for the play students at the Open Book wrote on the housing crisis), which could be an impetus toward collective political action. I would also recommend that more oral histories of the adult literacy community be published. Adult literacy students have powerful things to say, which demand to be heard. Oral history is one way for people to tell their own stories in their own voices.

In addition, we learn how the Open Book also provided a space that offered new ways of acting and being in the world. People described their classmates as their family. Cecilia says: "The Open Book became not just a place but a group of people interested in participating in the life of the community in general." John adds, "We wanted an atmosphere that was more like a group of friends sitting around a table in someone's kitchen." Students stayed after class to work with other students. They discovered their words and actions impacted the culture of the program in ways both visible and invisible. If this place, this space in South Brooklyn, represented a microcosm of society, a different way of people being with each other that was rooted in a more humane vision of the world where equity and collectivity were the cornerstones and where treating each other with dignity and respect was as critical as the air we breathed, what are the larger implications?

In chronicling the reality of the Open Book and the multiple stories that lived within the layered multitextual history, I was simultaneously unpacking my own personal history regarding schooling and self-blame rooted in the dominant culture and ideologies. Without any option, many others and I were knowledge consumers of concepts and realities that were oppressive and toxic, many of which we internalized to our own detriment (Fanon, 1967; Memmi, 1965). The concept of reality is socially constructed by particular groups, who by intertextually explaining and interpreting reality at a particular moment are given the privilege (whether earned or not) of authoring a text. This idea was something that was never acknowledged (let alone deconstructed). I never even considered the notion of truth as conceptually provisional, particular, and subjective. In school, I felt researched on, not with. I, like millions of other schoolchildren who fell outside of the norm, internalized this failure, blaming myself for this negative experience. Parts of my self still continue to wear the invisible scars of the banking system. Almost imperceptibly, as with Antonia, Hazel, Aida, Earle, and Edami, this perception impacted my sense of who I was—my social identity. It has taken many years but I have come to acknowledge the construction of the scars embedded in the ridges of my consciousness and how damaging the school system has been to so many people's psyches (Luttrell, 1997). When I first heard students' stories so similar to my own of the pain inflicted by schooling, part of myself learned to question and unpack the culture of schooling, though the internalized scars of these experiences continue to haunt my perception of identity and self. Listening to Edami's, Hazel's, Antonia's, Earle's, Aida's, Yolanda's, and all of the other stories, I keenly felt the urgency for the world of adult literacy to undergo a transformation. Adult literacy education required unpacking how various pieces of oppression (race, class, gender) take hold of us in different ways (Luttrell, 1997). In spaces such as the Open Book, hope and transformation can flourish, as evidenced by the many stories of people who were able to redefine and renegotiate their own perceptions of possibilities and worlds. It is not enough to study reading and writing. We must also ask, for what purpose?

As a field, we must develop adult education practices that respectfully legitimize learners' lives, perspectives, discourses, and voices. This must begin with themes that students have generated (see Chapter 3 for the play on the housing crisis "Welcome Back, Lucy"). We legitimize learners' lives when we scrutinize the concept of constructedness in classrooms, when we acknowledge that all texts are someone's constructions, all reflect someone's point of view, privilege certain interests and agendas. Hemphill (2001) says that engaging students in scrutinizing their own texts and then scrutinizing the power structures in place in society could be valuable in beginning to unpeel notions of constructed identities, oppression, and otherness (p. 24). This examination can support students' agency in deconstructing arbitrary realities and the truths imposed by dominant ideologies. Connecting classrooms to specific contexts offers space for students to construct their own localized truths and reject grand narratives that don't reflect their everyday realities. Students can write their own narratives, which capture their own lived realities in all their dichotomies and contradictions.

Like the Open Book, community programs should scrutinize issues surrounding inequities as a central component of instruction. Only then can invisible norms be disrupted. By developing themes (codes) based on students' realities, where students' knowledge is legitimized instead of further marginalized, the dynamic can begin to shift. But we need to remember that we live in a society where dominant ideologies have set the invisible center and all voices are not afforded equal weight and legitimacy (Sparks and Peterson, 2000). In what ways is there hope for relationships grounded in integrity and mutuality to be developed where there are already built-in autocratic dynamics, where the knowledge students bring to the classroom is questioned, ignored, and devalued? (Sparks and Peterson, 2000). To what extent did the Open Book and other programs built on similar principles subvert that dynamic? To what extent is it possible to connect literacy programs that honor the history of social movements to other social justice struggles and form partnerships grounded in the struggle for a more humane, lovelier world? To what extent can those partnerships change and disrupt the direction of the field? As Horton emphatically states, the answers can only come from the people. We must listen to what students have to say and find ways in programs to reflect and build on those words, dreams, hopes, and desires. As a field we desperately need to explicitly connect issues of social inequity and injustice to adult literacy education and have the issue of social justice be the very foundation on which every program is built. It is no question that literacy programs are part of a much larger picture of economic inequity, capitalism, racism, and other forms of oppression (Hoyles, 1977). If we wish our society to be different, we need to be part of that change, to work in partnerships rooted in solidarity, not charity. It is no longer a choice but a necessity. We must work toward creating fairer, more equitable spaces, where more voices can be heard and we must listen to what those voices are saying.

In chronicling this oral history of the Open Book, we, the co-constructors of this story, have attempted to tell a "better story." As Luttrell (1997) states, better stories recognize oppression, clarify power relations, and outline the costs of alternative actions. Telling the type of story that unfolds in this document is a political act, which depends upon a community of supportive listeners, people who can read the stories in ways that neither blame nor discredit the words and their authenticity.

We have reached the final chapter of this story. But it is not the end. It may be finished, but it still lives on! The story of struggle and injustice is still continuing: threads in the fabric highlighting inequities and silencing of voices have yet to emerge, those voices have yet to speak and be listened to. We have shared with you our constructed journey of the Open Book; we, who represented the multifaceted history of the program, its beginning, its struggles, its end, and its living impact. However, this story is part of a broader context, one that involves institutionalized economic inequities directed at poor communities, rooted in racism, silencing, and the continuous onslaught of stripping certain segments of our society of their basic human rights and dignity. In reading this story of the Open Book, we ask you to collectively scrutinize dominant ideologies shaping people's realities, question those realities, and reject them.

Come together and share your story, as we did ours. On some days, the power of a good story has the ability to sustain us more than food and drink ever could. We hope that this is such a story. As Coles (1989) points out, people come to us with stories that represent their lives. They hope they tell these stories well enough so we understand certain truths about their lives, and they hope we know how to interpret those stories accurately. In literacy education, as in much of "dominant culture," all too often what is engaged in is an expert problem-solving approach to viewing adult literacy students and "othered" segments of our population with preconceived notions of what does and doesn't matter. Instead of providing the space for students' stories to unfold, we're likely to rush in with labels; we're the experts, after all. We scarcely pause at the messages omitted, yarns gone untold, details brushed aside together, so rushed are we to get to the conclusion. Stories—yours, mine—we all carry them with us on this journey we take and we owe it to each other to honor and cherish those stories and learn from them (Coles, 1989, pp. 14–21).

Our Words Still Live On!
Dianne Ramdeholl

Beyond emotions
gestures and senses
lies a world
where our stories reside
words nestled against one another
cherished and cherishing
we will meet
will come together
in spaces between letters, syllables, words, sentences, and punctuation
tracing patterns of shared history
on the ground
all around us
we sprinkle words and anecdotes
vignettes and parables
our co-story.
Marking a trail,
symbolizing a collective journey traveled.
For all who have come before and will come after
and for ourselves
should we get lost
or lose each other.

APPENDIX A

The Shaping of This Story

Falling in Love with One's Data
Dianne Ramdeholl

Defenses slowly crumble
falling to the ground
Intense vulnerability overcomes me
cloaking me in an inability to think or respond
I look away
Seeking solace
hiding from your gaze
In your presence
I seem devoid of
language, thought or emotion.

But inwardly
Oh, inwardly
A furnace of ideas
catch and blaze in my head
kindling and fueling each other
at lightning speed
Volcanoes of questions erupt
I listen to your words over and over and over again
until they're permanently
imprinted and etched in my brain
I deeply inhale your speech rhythms
your pauses, your uh-huhs, and ums
Even asleep I can identify
your thought patterns

Somehow I/you
made space in my heart and
you took up residence in my bones
walking in and out of my thoughts and dreams
Your words recount
past and current struggles and lived experiences
weaving themselves into a
robe of magic
which warms me
filling me with visions of
hope, courage, and possibility
for each battle that must be fought
Dates, timelines, names, conversations
help me better understand and
honor your beautiful, complex essence
Should I attempt to theorize you
or classify you by labels
would cause you to leave and disappear
Instead, I must find you with
my eyes and heart
So I pick up my pencil
And learn to live
in the eye of the storm.

In February 2005, on a sunny but cold wintry afternoon with traces of the last snowfall still visible on the ground, ten people (students and teachers of varying socioeconomic and racial backgrounds) came together and resoundingly decided that the story of the Open Book was one that needed to be told. Throughout the course of the following year, sixteen of us met in small groups ranging from three to eight people for a total of ten conversations rooted in the Open Book's history. These conversations, which lasted for a total of over thirty hours, took place mostly in homes. Each time we met, the mood would shift, become more focused, more intense, and suddenly, without any warning we were back in that space where love, community, and each other became the air we breathed. I was incredulous at how effortlessly the magic would flare up among us. Is this how it would always be? In our meetings, there was always food and rich dialogue that never ended before three hours had passed.

Throughout many of the conversations and indeed much of the process, I was assailed by feelings that I had no right to do this, to listen to the sacredness and intimacy of people's words and stories and then use it as "just data." What if I couldn't chronicle this history in ways that someone who had lived and breathed it for its entire duration could? What if I couldn't convey the power of these stories in ways that honored the spirit in which they were told? But somewhere, somehow along the process, I began to internalize the stories, to understand them in whole new ways and to be more aware of the connections they had to my own life. I listened to them over and over again, and they inserted themselves into my dreams and consciousness. I began living with these stories, began wearing them until they seeped through the pores of my skin and flowed into my bloodstream.

I also became more fully conscious that as a woman of Indian, British, and Tibetan ancestry who was born and spent her childhood in a former colony (Guyana), the story of certain Open Book students shared important commonalities with many Guyanese people; indeed my own great-grandmother was an indentured immigrant from India who wasn't a proficient reader or writer. Through this process, I became increasingly awakened to the multiple ways in which this story emerged from who I was, who I am, and who I have yet to become. I should also add that in large part, because I had worked at the Open Book, many people saw me as an insider. As a result, the conversations were grounded in a level of richness and complexity that I am certain would have been absent otherwise.

In reading over and listening to people's words again and again, I kept thinking of possible shapes the final product could take that would support the urgency and agency of people's stories, and all of the other stories that resided in corners of yet more stories—all of which could easily take a lifetime to chronicle. I instinctively rejected models that would use people's words as a supportive backdrop to enforce my statements. If I were to honor these stories in meaningful ways, I needed to treat people's words with the dignity that was an inherent aspect of the Open Book.

From the very beginning, I could see and feel the richness of people's words, and I knew they were complete enough to stand on their own. After all, who could better tell the story of a program but the group of people who had lived and were at the center of the story? The decision to include the conversations that would eventually find their way into the text was essentially an intuitive process. I selected representative moments that reflected important aspects of the history. These seemed to be important because people returned repeatedly to further grapple, question, probe, and process. Important events in the program's timeline also found their way into the story. Throughout the process, I checked with the other co-constructors, inquiring whether the chapters reflected critical elements of the Open Book's story. They felt they did.

Appendix B

Welcome Back, Lucy

An Introduction

Good morning. This is a play about housing. It takes place in our neighborhood on Eighth Street in Park Slope (Brooklyn, New York). It is a play about a landlord who is trying to evict tenants. He wants to convert the building into co-ops, something that the tenants can't afford. It is an eight-unit building, which means the tenants qualify for certain rights. The play begins when some tenants meet in the lobby.

Mrs. Brown is a senior citizen. She has lived in the building for twenty years. Everyone likes her.

Mary Johnson came from Haiti with her two children. She lived in the building for eight years. She is a strong person, a real doozy.

Lucy is a nice person, but she is always afraid of everything, including the welfare. She lived in the building for seven years with her six children.

Scene 1: Mary, Lucy, and Mrs. Brown in the Lobby

Mary: Hi, Mrs. Brown, how are you?

Mrs. Brown: Hi, Mary, I'm fine.

Mary: Mrs. Brown, the landlord sent me a letter saying he wants me out. He tells me that my kids are always running in the hallway. But I don't let them do that. I always take care of my children. When they come in after school, they always have something to do. He complain about my dog. He says he's going to evict me. Mrs. Brown, what do you think I should do?

Mrs. Brown: You know the building has been very nice. But seems like it kind of went downhill. It's not clean any more. Everything is very rundown.

Mary: I always pay my rent. He don't have respect. He's supposed to fix my apartment. I have roaches, no heat. The bathroom is leaking, the paint is peeling from the ceiling. Now he gives me complaint. I'm going to keep my rent and make a letter. I'll take him to housing court. He has to change his mind, because I'm not going to let him put me down. You know something else, Mrs. Brown? The landlord, he's fresh. One day, it was hot. I go out by myself. He come up behind me. He say, "You have big breasts."

Mrs. Brown: You know Lucy, the girl in the second floor? She got a letter like that, too. She's very scared.

Mary: Who's Lucy?

Mrs. Brown: She's the girl on the second floor. The nervous girl. She's nervous about getting evicted.

Mary: That's no good. If you let these people get in your blood, you in trouble.

(Lucy comes walking into the lobby. She has a letter in her hand and she seems kind of nervous.)

Lucy: Mrs. Brown, here's that letter I told you about. I don't know what to do, I'm scared.

Mary: Why are you scared? You come from here, you're American. You know the law.

Lucy: I don't know the law. Just because you're American, doesn't mean you know the law. You don't really have any rights. When you're on welfare, you gotta do what they say.

Mary: You don't have to do what they say. You can fight back.

Lucy: That's easy for you to say. The welfare doesn't give you problems. My social worker does. She tells me to pay the rent no matter what shape the apartment is in.

Mary: What are you going to do? Go to a shelter? Not me. I'm not garbage. I'm going to stay right here. Let's fight for this. Keep our apartments.

Mrs. Brown: I think we need to have a meeting in the building. A meeting of all the tenants. Let's call a meeting.

Come to a Tenant Meeting
On Wednesday at 7:30 p.m.
At Mrs. Brown's Apartment, 1A
Coffee and Cake will be Served.

It is important to attend this meeting referring to the letter everyone has received and the co-ops that they want to bring to our building.

Scene 2: In the Landlord's Office

Mrs. Brown: Where's Lucy?

Ms. Smith: She couldn't make it. Where's the landlord, anyway?

Mrs. Brown: I don't know.

Lou: It's 5:30, are you sure he said 4:30?

Ms. Smith: Yes.

Lou: This is ridiculous. A whole hour. It doesn't make sense.

Secretary: He's late for everything.

Ms. Smith: We came all this way.

Mrs. Brown: Maybe he had something to do.

Lou: Yeah, like playing golf or something like that.

(All of a sudden, the landlord walks into the office.)

Landlord: How you doing everybody? Sorry I'm a little late but you know how traffic is. What can I do for you?

Ms. Smith: Well, we had a tenants' meeting, and we got a lot of complaints about the building, and we would like you to do something about them. Mary Johnson has a hole in the ceiling. It leaks down into her bathroom. Also we ...

Landlord: Excuse me, Mrs. Johnson, but I've sent a man over there to fix that ceiling a couple of times, and you have not been there.

Mary Johnson: That's not true. I'm always home during the day.

Landlord: So when can we come to fix it?

Mary Johnson: You can come anytime. Just let me know when you're going to be there.

Landlord: So where's the water coming from?

Mary Johnson: From Lucy's apartment.

Landlord: Have you been up to Lucy's apartment? What does she have, a machine or something?

Mary Johnson: No, she has a leak from her bathroom.

Landlord: I've sent someone over there to look at it. She's never home.

Mary Johnson: She's always home. Are you kidding?

Landlord: Look, Mrs. Brown's been living there for twenty years. Mrs. Brown, when you moved in there, wasn't that a nice apartment? Nice and clean and everything. And the building was nice and clean, too.

Mrs. Brown: Yes, but these days it's terrible.

Landlord: Well, these days the people who are living there never take care of it.

Ms. Smith: But, we do take care of it.

Landlord: I mean, the garbage is always in the hallways, people are hanging out inside the building ...

Ms. Smith: That's because the lock on the door is not there.

Landlord: I've fixed that door many times. Every time I fix that door it's broken.

Lou: That door's like cardboard. How much did you pay for it, $20?

Landlord: Well, I can't put brass on it cos that's going to cost me a lot of money. But I'll tell you what. I'll fix the door this time, but the next time I fix the door it's going to come out of your rent.

Mary Johnson: That's what you think!

Mrs. Brown: We can't afford that.

Landlord: I can't afford it either.

Ms. Smith: Look, we need a decent door with a good lock and an intercom.

Landlord: An intercom! Where do you people think you live, on Park Avenue? I don't even have that in my building. In a little while you're going to want elevators. You must think I'm a millionaire.

Ms. Smith: Look, we pay our rent every month ...

Landlord: Some people pay their rent every month. But some people don't pay their rent on time.

Lou: What is this we hear about co-ops?

Landlord: Well, right now I don't know what I'm going to do, whether I'm going to make it into co-ops right now. But if I do, believe me, you'll be the first to know.

Lou: Oh, thanks.

Landlord: Right now, I don't even know what I'm going to do. I'm having problems with this house constantly, broken windows, broken doors, cracks in the ceilings ... who's doing all this?

Ms. Smith: Look, it's your responsibility to fix these things, and you haven't been doing it.

Landlord: Okay, we're going to send a plumber to the house on Monday at 2 o'clock.

Mrs. Smith: Are you going to be there?

Mary Johnson: I'll be there. I'll be there all day.

Ms. Smith: Are you going to fix the front door and the bells?

Landlord: How many times do I have to fix them? It's too much.

Mrs. Brown: Listen, we need our bells fixed. We pay our rent. I'm on social security.

Landlord: Okay, I'll do it this time, but I'm not making any promises about the future.

Ms. Smith: What about the co-op? You never answered our question about the co-ops.

Landlord: I'm sorry. I have to leave now. I have another appointment. If you have any more questions, leave them with my secretary.

(The landlord gets up and leaves. Everyone else sits there in silence for 10 or 15 seconds.)

Ms. Smith: What happened?

Lou: What did he do?

Mary Johnson: He didn't do anything.

Mrs. Brown: We'll just have to keep on fighting, that's all.

(All the tenants get up and leave. As they're leaving, Mary Johnson says to the secretary, "We'll be back.")

Scene 3: Lucy Comes Back to Visit

Ms. Smith: How are you making it, girl?

Lucy: Not very good. I listened to the landlord. He said he'd get me another apartment, but now I'm at the shelter.

Mrs. Brown: We told you we'd help you. Why didn't you come to us?

Lucy: I didn't listen. I was afraid. I should have stayed here. I should have listened to what you said. I should have listened to what Mary said. Now they want to take my kids away. The first two days I was in the park. I'm begging people on the streets for a quarter. You have to sleep with one eye open, one eye closed. Sometimes you sleep on a roof, sometimes underneath a trailer. Now you're out on the street, you don't know what you're doing. You're out there picking up stuff from the street every night, sleeping under trailers. You don't know when someone might rape you. A cop saw me crying. The children were hungry. The cop took me to the shelter. It's not real nice, but at least the kids have something to eat. Everyone sleeps in one big room. All the cots are together, there's no privacy. You have to watch your kids. Sometimes men use the women's bathrooms.

(All of a sudden there's a knock on the door.)

Mrs. Brown: Come in.

(The door opens, and all the other tenants walk in.)

Everybody: Hey, Lucy! Lucy, how you doing? Welcome back, Lucy!

(Everybody comes together around Lucy and hugs her. Then they all join hands on the table.)

Narrator: This is happening to thousands of people: the poor and the middle class are being driven out of their homes; children are being taken out of schools. It's happening to a lot of people, and we should keep fighting.

This play was written by students in the Open Book program in the mid-1980s and used by students at the Open Book for many years after that.

Appendix C

I Developed a Way of Looking at People
Angel Ruiz

I came to this country from Puerto Rico when I was one year old. My mother and my father decided to come to this country because in those days it was hard for them to support a family. Labor was cheap. My father and my mother started working here and for the first five years of my life, everything was going normal.

But then, when I was five years old, my father, when he took me to school, detected something was wrong with me. My parents took me to the hospital and they found out that I had polio when I was a little kid. So, for the first two to three years after that, I couldn't go to school because I was constantly inside the hospitals. In those days it was hard to get somebody to tutor people in the hospital. So, for the next six years of this time I lost a lot of touch with school: with reading and writing. And I lost touch with feeling with other people and how to relate to other people.

So, when I was around seven years old, I decided to make my own self, find a way to communicate with other people. What happened was, during the years, up to like eighteen years old, I was in and out of hospitals. I had twenty-two operations. What I did was I developed a way of looking at people, at the way they talk. I picked up their way of doing things, like the way they use their hands, the way they would talk to another person. Or if they were talkin' about some books that they were reading, I would watch how they would talk, at their image. Yeah, they would talk about, like some nurses would read books, like love stories and I used to watch them. Or I would sit with them and watch the way they would talk and explain what their feeling about the person in the book was. And then I would pick that up. What I picked up from other people, I would get into a conversation. I said, "Well, that's a nice book." I would try to do the same thing like the other people did.

I was covering for myself. Because I was afraid that if they would find out I couldn't read and write that they would just back away from me. So, what I did was

I would try to imitate everybody else and be into, get into the group and try to fit into society. At the same time I developed certain ways of doing writing. I used to ask people, "I remember this word but sometimes people write it different ways. Will you tell me how you write it?" And I would get the person to write the word without me letting them know that I couldn't read it or write it. So they would write it down on a piece of paper and say, "That's the right way." And then I would write and say, "This is the way I write it." Which I never did!

I used to be in the hospital for six months, then go home and go to school for maybe eight or nine months, and then end up back in the hospital. So I could never finish school. I used to live around Delancey Street in Manhattan, on the Lower East Side. I grew up in a neighborhood where mostly everybody was junkies falling on the stairs, under the doors, they were dying. I always said to myself that I would never see myself like that. I couldn't see myself living that kind of life! I went through pain and I saw these people's faces and I couldn't see myself goin' through all that agony in life.

Back in school, in the classes were so many kids, like 50 kids, 40 kids and one teacher. I did go to auto mechanic school. I finished my first two years and then after that I couldn't finish because then the doctors told me I had to go into the hospital again and it would take me at least two years to recuperate. So, for those two years when I was in the hospital constantly, I had nobody to come in and help me out. I would talk to the other patients and give them my feelings about life. I felt, you know, I went through the whole pain routine and I would relate to them like an older person to an older person. I grew up with older persons constantly. I was never in a ward with younger people. So when I went outside to relate to younger people or when I went to school, I was afraid that I couldn't understand a lot of the stuff that they did. So I developed a way of doing my thing without nobody knowing what was wrong with me. But then, I started working, in 1969, in the gold business. Everything was supposed to be written down on pieces of paper. So what I did was I'd get somebody to write everything up and I would do it by mind. When they read instructions to me I would draw it. If they told me, "You have to file a ring," I would draw a picture of a person doing a filing and I would know that would be question 1. Or, if they would tell me the ring has to be sized to a bigger size, I would make a picture of a ring and then cut it. Like make believe it was supposed to be bigger or smaller. Everything I would put in pictures. My routine was everything in pictures or in numbers. I had certain numbers and I would remember number 1 was this or number 2 was that. I never did writing.

During the years I got away with it. But then, for the last five or six years, everything has been changing. Everything's becoming computerized. Everything has to be written to go into a computer. I couldn't get away with routine no more. So now what I did was to get other people to write down words. I would put all those words on a piece of paper. And I would keep them in my drawer. When I needed that word I would pick it out and write it down. And I still do that. Like I picked up a certain line of words and I know I have to use the same line so I learned those words. When I have to write something, I know what I have to write down. Because I already know the routine of the job. I know those words now because I've been constantly workin' with those words. This way, when I put it into the computer it was written by my hand. So they don't realize I can't read or write!

I got married seven years ago. My wife Ana, she worked for the Board of Education. She's a well-educated woman and she started pushin' me. She said that I needed to do something in life for me and for the kids.

About four years ago I was lookin' for a school program. But it was hard to find a program to help the handicapped and help out the people who can't read and write. So I tried a lot of programs and I couldn't find one that fit my needs. So I let it go. Two years ago I saw this program on T.V. where they said that people were losin' jobs and this nation is losin' jobs because people can't read and write. I knew I was one of them and that story related to me. I found this [Open Book] program about a year and a month ago.

When I started here I was afraid that I couldn't fit in because I couldn't read and write, not hardly nothin'. I wanted to learn because I have two daughters and my oldest daughter, she's very smart and she's always askin' me too many questions. She reads a lot and she wants me to read books with her and everything. By learning how to read and write I wanted to help my daughter, and I'm gonna help myself and hopefully in the future I want to be a helper for other people. I could relate to others, people who had problems like I did. Handicapped people need more attention because they have problems and when they went to these programs nobody could understand what was wrong with them. In my own life I went through a lot of pain and going through all these routines, forcing myself to do things I didn't do—maybe I might help somebody else, maybe make it easier for them.

I feel like I'm holding my wife back too. Sometimes we sit down and talk and I see that she's got a lot of potential to do a lot of other stuff. She left her job because she wanted to be a mother to the kids. But sometimes I feel like I have made her completely lose touch with her career, her way of doing things. We sit down and sometimes we talk and I see in her that sometimes she's writing and she feels she loves to read a lot of books. Her sister gives her books, college stuff and I see that she loves all this and I feel like I'm holding her back from doing a lot of things that she wants to do. And sometimes I feel bad. So that's why I wanted to learn, it made me feel like I *have* to learn. Maybe she could go back to work and I think she'll feel better then.

If I got a better job it would take the pressure off her for doing everything with the kids. She has to do everything. Sometimes she gets mad because she doesn't have the time and then I feel like I'm, you know, I'm makin' her do everything. I feel like marriage has to be a 50-50 thing, you know, both of us. But right now I feel like she's doin' everything and I'm doin' nothin'. It makes me feel like I'm putting all the pressure on her. By learning how to read and write I would take away a lot of that pressure off of her. And maybe let her do something for herself. Let her go back to work and that would make her feel better because she'll probably be earning money and you know, getting stuff for herself. It's hard for us. I have offers for better jobs, but since I can't read and write, I can't take those jobs. And it's hard for her because it's tight, tight everywhere. That's budget-wise and what I make is not enough to support a family the way we want to.

She's been supportive for seven years, she's been pushin' me to do a lot of things. If it wasn't for her I don't think I would be here either. She says since I've been in school she has seen a big difference, a complete difference in me. I'm more aware of things and I'm more loose, you know. I'm not uptight like I used to be. I can talk more to her. I can relate more to her. Before I couldn't explain myself to her. My learning how to read some has made me feel easier to talk to her and made me feel more comfortable to relate to her. And now I can explain to her with words that I've picked up. It's easier and she can understand.

One year to me has made the difference for thirty-six years of my life. For thirty-six years I was like in a shell. I was tryin' to get out of that shell but I couldn't get out. I tried different ways but I was afraid that nobody would understand what was goin' on. Being here a year and a month has given me the confidence of letting myself loose and expressing myself. That is expressing myself for what I want and not be afraid of what comes after that. To go ahead and don't give up. To try something without having the fear that it will come out wrong. I push myself more now. If I do something wrong, I just keep working at it. Now I have the confidence that I can move forward and push myself more and more.

I don't have to keep things locked up inside me. Sometimes I dream, like I'm in this shell. And I can't get out of this shell and everybody is surrounding me and they're like torturing me because they say I'm a nobody. I have this fear that if I get out, break out of that shell, that everybody's not going to accept me for what I am or what I've accomplished. It's like they want me to stay in this shell because that's what I've been all my life, that that's what I will be for the rest of my life.

Sometimes I have nice dreams and sometimes it's just like torture. Sometimes I wake up and think, "Where am I?" and "Why? Why?" These dreams have helped me out with a lot of stuff too. This can show me a way out of a lot of the problems in life. Sometimes I dream that I'm walkin' in the air and there's no problem in life. But in reality, when I come down, I face what life is really all about and what's goin' on around me. What I have seen all of my life: poverty and poor people because I have lived between poor people, drugs, and problems. It's all over this country, all over this world, and I see so many things.

I feel I would like to do something. I would love to change something in life. I would love to help people out. I could help out younger people when they have problems with drugs. Or any kind of problems that people might have. And if I help somebody, that will also help me to build up my own skills and my own confidence that I could do something in life. The one year that I have here in school has made me just forget about the pains of before. It's a feeling like those thirty-five years of my past, it was just a dream. Like it never happened. Because it made me realize a lot of stuff I couldn't realize before.

Some people can fight and not give up. I guess it's just their way of thinking. If they think they are gonna be nobody, they will be a nobody! If they think that they can't get the help or that everything is just a NO—a negative to life, then they'll never get out. Because I grew up in a neighborhood where they had junkies, they had everything you could think of. That's why I say that it's in the individual. You got to search deep inside you, go look inside you and say to yourself, "I will never give up in life." Because there is always something better. You have to have will power. You have to have the strength, the inner strength. Even if you go to a psychiatrist, they could say, "You could do it, you could do it," but if you don't believe it, they ain't gonna help you.

I believe that I have one thing going for me. That is I believe that I can push myself. And I will never give up. I will fight until, I think, the last day of my life. This is like a dream that I'm gonna go ahead and I'm gonna accomplish what I want in life. For myself, for my family, for the world, for other people who need me. If I could help them out I would think that I had accomplished a lot in life. Sometimes in class I sit down, I talk with other people and I start reading with them. And I feel like when we're reading together we're accomplishing a lot. The other person helps me out with a word and I help them out with a word and that makes me feel good. Sometimes there are days when it's hard because there are a lot of things goin' on, but I can't give up.

Like I said, this one year and a month, to me has meant thirty-five years of my life. It's like freedom. Like a slave, I was a slave to myself, my inner self. That's what it is. I was locked into myself and I've been opening that shell and getting out of it. I've been spreading out, like a bird spreading out their wings, by picking up knowledge little by little.

I feel like somebody owned me and I couldn't be my own boss. Like somebody told me what to do and I had to do it. And that's all there was. There was nothing else in life. And I felt like that was sometimes like, what am I, a person or an animal? I felt sometimes like an animal, like I had to go to work and do my work, and that's it. Because that's all I was worth—to do my work and forget about everything else.

By learning a word, for me every word that I learn is something new in life. It's like flowers, every flower that opens makes everything more beautiful. So by learning, by even seeing a sentence, to me that sentence is worth millions of things to me. When I couldn't read or write, I felt like I couldn't explain myself. But by writing a sentence now, that sentence means more to me than anything else now. Like if I write a sentence—like sometimes I write to my wife: I love you and I miss you a lot. Right there, that means everything to me because that's my feeling I'm writing there. Before when I couldn't write my feelings it was frustrating to me. I couldn't write what I felt inside my heart. The only way I had to do it was by talking to a person, but I couldn't, I couldn't feel relaxed. Sometimes I couldn't get out that feeling that I had in my heart. I felt like if I knew how to write it, I could write down what I felt in my own way. That could make me feel like I'm expressing myself better, by writing. Sometimes I can't talk. If I talk to a person I get confused with certain words. If I write it down I feel more comfortable. I can write what I really feel.

Reading makes me feel more positive in life. It has made me feel stronger. It's like a novel—you turn one page and that page just keeps on moving. And the more I read, the more knowledge I'm pickin' up. And the more I can understand in life, the more things I can see that I missed a long time ago. It's helpin' me out in everything.

Like I said, it gives me more self-confidence. It has helped me to see things better, more clearer. By reading I can know what's goin' on with other people and what's goin' on in another part of the world. I can relate to those people's problems by reading. Because I grew up in poor neighborhoods and by reading about another poor neighborhood in another part of the world, that reading makes me feel what those people have been feeling in life. Not by looking at T.V.

T.V. just *shows* you. But if I read it, it gives me more of a feeling of what those people are going through—the agony and the pain. Yeah, it's the inner feelings because if a person writes about something that happens to them, if I read it I could relate to that person better. We read about people in the East Village, where they're all living in all those abandoned buildings, and by reading I know what they are going through. That's opening my eyes to what I have seen before. This helps me to understand more. My mind is opened. By seeing this ... we don't know our future—right now I might lose my job. I could be like one of these people, any of us could. By reading it and seeing it I have a better sense of what really goes on.

An earlier version appeared in *Four Stories* (Ruiz, 1989).

Appendix D

Welfare and Literacy

John Gordon

In the mountains of Nayarit in Mexico, there was a community that had no name. For centuries this community of Huichol Indians had been looking for a name. Carlos Gonzalez found one by sheer accident.

This Huichol had come to the city of Tepic to buy seeds and visit relatives. Crossing a garbage dump, he picked up a book thrown into the rubbish. It was years ago that Carlos had learned to read the Castilian language, and he could still just about manage it. Sitting in the shade of a projecting roof, he began to decipher the pages. The book spoke of a country with a strange name, which Carlos couldn't place but which had to be far from Mexico, and told a story of a recent occurrence.

On the way home, walking up the mountain, Carlos continued reading. He couldn't tear himself away from this story of horror and bravery. The central character of the book was a man who kept his word. Arriving at the village, Carlos announced euphorically: "At last we have a name!"

And he read the book aloud to everyone. This halting recital took him almost a week. Afterward, the hundred and fifty families voted. All in favor. Dancing and singing they performed the baptism.

So finally they have a name for themselves. This community bears the name of a worthy man who did not doubt at the moment of choice between treachery and death.

"I'm going to Salvador Allende," the wayfarers say now.

—Eduardo Galeano, *Century of the Wind* (1986)

Many of us came into adult education because we believed in the transformative power of adult education, because we believed that learning to read and write would not just open doors for some individuals but had the potential to give students the skills to understand and act on their world more effectively, to gain control over their lives, to act in concert with others to change the conditions of life in their communities. Implicit in this view was a notion that education itself was good, that by learning to read people would be opened up to new experiences and ideas, and in the process become different and perhaps more powerful people.

Like the campesino in Galeano's story, their reading would allow them to act on their world in ways which they had not dreamed of before. Carlos reads about events in a place he has never heard of. He is transfixed by the story, unable to tear himself away from the book. The story inspires him, perhaps allows him to see possibilities he hadn't imagined before. Carlos and his neighbors rename their community and, in a profound sense, redefine themselves.

I think that this belief in the potential of education to sponsor and provoke change, rather than the hope that we could help them get jobs (no matter how important that is) is what inspired many of us to become teachers. This article is about the way welfare is transforming the nature of literacy and English as a Second Language Classes in the city. But it is also about us—teachers, administrators, counselors—and our role in this process. It is about what we want to be doing and what we are doing.

Five years ago, the Office of Employment Services (OES) began to demand that Adult Basic Education (ABE) programs report student attendance. About once a month, OES sends each program a roster of its students on Public Assistance known to be receiving Training Related Expenses (TREs). TREs include transportation, childcare, and sometimes lunch money. Programs are expected to report on the attendance of the students listed in order to determine whether or not they should continue receiving their TREs. Students whose attendance is reported at less than seventy-five percent have their TREs cut immediately. No excuses are accepted. If a program fails to respond to the roster, all the students listed have their TREs cut off. If a program fails to return the roster for two months in a row, it is removed from the Master List of Approved Training Programs.

When we first began to receive the roster, it led us to reflect on a number of things. First and foremost was the question of how to respond so that students would not be hurt. Second, we wondered where it fit into impending welfare reform legislation. What would be required of programs and of recipients in the future? It led us to also reflect upon our role as educators. Most of us receive funding and support from institutions whose goals sometimes contradict our own. How do we respond to the demands of those institutions and still remain accountable to ourselves and to students? Who is to determine what we do when faced with this contradiction? As teachers and administrators, we realize that we have a responsibility to continually question whom we are actually serving. We have to challenge ourselves or fall victim to the bureaucracies that attempt to dictate to us and our students.

We were outraged by the rosters. First of all, seventy-five percent attendance (it was eighty percent at the time) is unrealistic as a "standard" for Adult Basic

Education students. Because of responsibilities outside of school, students are always juggling the pieces of their lives—childcare, sickness, meetings with welfare, housing concerns, etc. Only students themselves can determine how to most successfully work their school schedules into their lives. The real issue is whether or not people are learning to read and write at a rate that meets their needs.

Second, and most relevant, is the issue of trust. Most ABE students have had a difficult time in past school experiences and almost all bring with them a profound sense of alienation from and mistrust of the education system. Where programs have been successful in attracting and retaining students is where they have been able to establish an atmosphere of warmth and support, allowing students to feel free to expose their weaknesses, and where relationships of trust and confidence can grow among the students, staff and teachers—relationships that are able to break down that sense of alienation and mistrust which tends to govern relations between people and the institutions that "serve" them.

Our feeling is that if we took on the role of monitoring student attendance and if our reports could result in loss of benefits, we would be undermining the very relationships that we have worked so long and hard to build. People would begin to see us as a police arm of welfare, and their presence in class as coerced. Under these circumstances, many might not remain, and those that did, might not trust enough to learn.

We were troubled at what appeared to be acceptance of this policing role on the part of other programs. Was it because people were too busy with other things to deal with this? Did others not see the broader implications of these rosters? Was there a sense of powerlessness among educators in the face of the massive welfare bureaucracy? Was everyone just planning to lie?

Although the rosters seemed to come out of nowhere, there was actually some advance notice. For us, the issue first came up at a meeting of program managers held by the Community Development Agency (CDA) in August 1987. At that meeting, David Hepinstall, then Assistant Commissioner of CDA, said that OES might be willing to make Training Related Expenses available to people on welfare who were attending ABE programs, but that the programs were going to have to be willing to report attendance. Someone objected, and Hepinstall's response was interesting and straightforward.

Essentially, he said the reason there is so much money for literacy available now is that there is a strong consensus among funders, policymakers, and corporate leaders that the United States economy is in bad shape, that it is no longer competitive on the world market, and that a big part of the problem is the low level of literacy in the workforce. Their strategy, then, is to get people off welfare and back to work as quickly as possible. They believe this means not only teaching people to read and write, but also educating them to the necessity of going to work.

Therefore, according to Hepinstall, funders were not going to budge on an issue like this, because they feel that people need to learn to accept the kind of externally imposed discipline that one finds in the world of work. What he did not say, but which seems patently obvious, is that this strategy involves the vast majority of the people in our programs learning to accept degrading jobs at low wages.

So, in January 1989, the Open Book, The Reading Council, and Bronx Educational Services decided that we had to challenge the rosters. We met with Donald Freedman, an attorney specializing in welfare issues, wrote to then Deputy Commissioner Cathy Zall, and arranged a meeting with her. We discussed among ourselves our goal. Ideally, it was to completely do away with the rosters. If this was not feasible (we did recognize the need of welfare to account for its money), we wanted to do away with any externally defined standard of acceptable attendance.

In the meeting with Cathy Zall, we focused on the need for trust in our programs and on the threat that these rosters posed. We talked about the eighty percent figure and suggested that it was unreasonable and irrelevant. What was more relevant was whether or not public assistance recipients were attending classes enough to be making progress in meeting their goals—learning how to read and write. The meeting went well and to our surprise, Ms. Zall basically agreed to our suggestions. The new rosters would have a column that said "satisfactory attendance and progress" with no reference to a specific percentage. In exchange, we agreed to report any significant change in a student's schedule. Ms. Zall felt she needed some means of distinguishing between programs and decided that the new procedure would be for CDA-funded agencies only. This may be because CDA and OES are both part of HRA. It is more likely that it is because all three organizations represented in the meeting were CDA-funded. A very simple lesson in organizing: when you speak up, you have a chance to make a difference.

In a follow-up letter to our lawyer, Ms. Zall said that it might take time for the headings on the rosters to change, but CDA-sponsored programs could make the changes themselves in the interim. With very little effort on our parts, we were able to effect a change on something significant in its own right and significant, also, in its broader implications.

In the years since then, our small victory has eroded. The headings on the rosters were never changed, though the eighty percent was reduced to seventy-five percent. We implemented the changed policy ourselves. OES has slowly gotten its act together, and, despite the fact that Ms. Zall is generally acknowledged to be liberal and enlightened, has demanded more and more. The forms have become more precise; rosters come more often. Threatening letters arrive from the OES office. Students are told that they must have fifteen hours of classes despite the fact that the programs they attend are not funded to offer that many hours.

On top of this, OES started its own adult education program, called BEGIN, specifically for students on public assistance. Some community-based organizations, as well as the City University system, are running their own BEGIN programs or EDGE programs. (EDGE is another program only for students on public assistance.) Both of these programs further isolate and ghettoize welfare recipients. Their entrance into the program, their attendance, and departure are coerced.

Then last spring, some English Speakers of Other Languages (ESOL) students began receiving notices from OES saying that they were no longer eligible for training related expenses because they had been in their programs too long (two years). At the same time, the State Department of Social Services (DSS) began to demand the right to make unannounced visits to ABE and ESOL programs to see classes and inspect student records.

There is certainly more to come. In fact, the state intends to replace the current attendance verification system (the rosters) with a "card swipe" system. They plan to install credit card–like boxes at each program, and when students arrive at school in the morning, they will run their card through the box and their arrival would be automatically recorded at HRA. A pilot project is beginning this year in New York City and Erie County, and, according to DSS, a lot of programs have signed on.

All of these developments take place in a climate in which welfare recipients are increasingly being cast as scapegoats. President Clinton has made welfare reform one of the central tenets of his program. It is Clinton, in fact, who has given legitimacy to the notion that people should only be on welfare for two years. Here in New York City, Mayor Giuliani, by demanding that public assistance recipients be fingerprinted, has set the stage for a kind of criminalization of people on welfare.

Students have reacted angrily to these developments. At the Open Book, many students talked about the way they are mistreated by the welfare system, that "just because they give you some money they think they can run your life." They felt it was ridiculous to expect someone to gain proficiency in a language or become a good reader in two years. Moreover, they felt the unannounced visits were degrading and an invasion of privacy. When one Open Book student heard about the card swipe system, she said, "Why don't they just put those ankle bracelets on you, like the ones they use for people on house arrest? Then they'll always know where we are."

Students in five or six programs organized meetings in their schools and traveled to other boroughs to hold joint meetings. In those meetings they came up with three demands: no time limits on participation to adult education programs, no more rosters, no unannounced visits by the State Department of Social Services.

We tend to regard welfare's demands as an unwelcome intrusion into the educational process, but for funders and policymakers they are part of the same package. Whatever our intentions are, literacy funding is primarily directed not at providing people with an education but at getting people off the welfare rolls. It is aimed not so much at education, but at re-education; not so much at giving people the academic and intellectual tools they need to better control their destiny, to understand and deal with the society we live in, but rather to change their attitudes, to convince them that they have no choice but to take a job, no matter how bad, no matter how low-paying, no matter how personally unfulfilling.

Many students could go out and get a minimum wage job at McDonald's or some other such place, but they do not. Why? Because the jobs are degrading, because there would be no health insurance, because they are smart enough to know that for them it does not pay. People resist bad choices. The function and purpose of adult literacy funding is, more than anything else, to break down that resistance. This direction, this orientation in literacy policy has been straightforward, out in the open and clearly stated for a long time.

The worst part about it is that we in the adult education community have not only acquiesced to these developments, we have accepted the basic assumptions behind welfare reform and incorporated them into our curricula and program designs. We have become cops for the welfare system.

The only protest I have heard with any consistency is about the amount of time and effort that goes into filling out forms and other types of paperwork. Some have argued that we should demand to be paid for this time.

I agree there is an enormous amount of time wasted in filling out these forms but I think if our strategy is to ask to be paid for the time, we, in essence, buy into the system. We put our stamp of approval on it; in fact we begin to benefit from it because our salaries will then be paid partly by these funds. And this is the problem—our reactions to the encroachments of welfare have been shaped and conditioned by our positions as administrators, teachers, and counselors. We see the issues from the perspective of people who are inside the system and have a stake in its continuance, rather than from the perspective of the people who are outside, the students themselves.

The logic of the debate is always set by the needs and prerogatives of the system itself. The government insists that if it is going to be paying out millions of dollars every year in carfare and childcare expenses, then it has the right to make sure that the money is being spent where it is supposed to be. Well, yes. But then again, what about the students' perspective? What about their right to respect, dignity, and autonomy?

I would argue that these funding initiatives and welfare reforms are inherently oppressive, designed to regain control over a workforce that is, in a certain sense, in rebellion. Let me ask a question. How many of the people who are in the BEGIN program would really rather not be there? For that matter, how many public assistance recipients in the other ABE and ESOL programs would rather not be there? I do not pretend to know the answer to those questions, but I do think that if the answer is "a lot," then these programs would be better off closed.

Some will undoubtedly feel attacked by my arguments, but my purpose is not to attack. These are confusing issues, and the alternatives are not all that clear. But I think we all need to take a good hard look at what we are doing. We need to think not only about what adult education is, but what it is in the process of becoming. From the point of view of students on public assistance, how much difference is there between BEGIN and another program? How much difference will there be in a year? We need to listen to the students. We need to develop some unity around these issues. We need to figure out how we can have an impact on literacy policy. We have to expand our focus from "how much" to "what" and "why."

And we have to make some choices. Our choices are not nearly so stark or so clear as the choice that faced Salvador Allende. Certainly no one is going to name a town after us. But perhaps we still have time to write a good book!

Sections of this article are excerpted from an unpublished manuscript by John Gordon and Barbara Gross (Spring 1990).

John Gordon was the director of the Open Book, a community-based organization in Brooklyn.

Appendix E

Zigs and Zags

Doing Literacy in the Era of WIA

John Gordon

For the last fifteen years, I have been the teacher-coordinator of the Open Book, a community based A.B.E. program in Brooklyn, New York. The Open Book was founded by Good Shepherd Services in 1985 during the wave of literacy funding that launched many New York City programs. From the beginning we saw our mission as creating a center where people could come and learn the kinds of things they felt they needed to learn to improve their lives and the lives of others in their families and communities.

We have worked hard during these fifteen years to build a program based on the needs of our student body. The program has had several key characteristics: a high degree of student involvement in decision-making, a curriculum built on the themes and concerns articulated by the students themselves, a focus on writing and publishing, and a strong sense of community within the school. We have seen the publishing both as a way to provide texts that reflect the voices, issues, and concerns students bring to the program as well as a way to foster dialogue and study around those issues.

We have focused particularly on trying to build a democratic community within the school, so that the values and culture of the Open Book would be defined largely by the students and the educational program would respond to the real goals of the student body. This has been an imperfect process, littered with struggles and difficulties, errors and confusions. It has been at the same time a very exciting project, one that we feel has resulted in an atmosphere of tremendous personal and collective growth, one in which students have felt valued and affirmed, and, of course, one in which many, many people have learned to read and write better and transformed their sense of themselves.

We know we have a lot to learn about how people learn to read and write, about assessment, about teaching math, about almost every area of our work. We need, for example, to get better at helping people take what they've learned out of the school and into the community. Indeed, I would love to focus this paper on the questions and issues that we debate in staff meetings and schoolwide meetings: on how to adjust to the large numbers of young people coming in to the school, on the informal book group we started as a transition to college last spring, on making sense of the articles that our staff read on teaching math last year, and so on.

But the truth is that as we enter the 2000–2001 school year, I fear for the survival of the Open Book and others like us.

The signs have been there for some time. In 1989 the welfare system imposed itself upon us, insisting that we report to them when welfare recipients attending our programs had "unsatisfactory" attendance. Students failing to meet their standards were sanctioned. We, in effect, became an arm of the state welfare apparatus, really part of a system of social control, thereby threatening the relationship of trust between student and teacher that is central to our mission.

Then in 1996, they took it one step further, mandating that students on public assistance attend literacy programs twenty hours per week if they wanted to keep receiving their checks. Many literacy programs were forced to restructure to provide the necessary hours. But that phase was short-lived, because the following year, in the wake of President Clinton's Welfare Reform Act, designed to end welfare (and, in retrospect, literacy) as we knew it, it was decided that welfare recipients didn't need to go to school at all. They should just go straight to work. En masse, literacy programs lost a key part of their student body as welfare recipients were forced out of school and into workfare programs. We were told that we had to cut our classes to no more than fifteen hours per week so welfare recipients would have time to clean the streets. It felt a bit like literacy was the tail being wagged by welfare policy.

These zigzags grew out of the view on the part of policy-makers that the central purpose of literacy funding (and welfare policy) is workforce development—that is, making the economy more productive.

Now we have the Workforce Investment Act, which by folding adult education into workforce development has enshrined this tendency into law, and along with it a series of accountability measures and performance goals designed to ensure that literacy programs across the country turn their attention to job placement. Elsewhere in this issue, there is a detailed analysis of where WIA is leading us, so I won't try to do that here. But I do want to make a couple of points.

When legislators in Washington pass laws like the Workforce Investment Act, I don't believe it's because they think the best way to help undereducated people is to help them find jobs. Rather they are encouraged by corporate leaders and economic think tanks, looking at ways to bring down the high cost of labor and make cheap labor more plentiful. Their view is that there are hundreds of thousands of undereducated, unemployed people who could be working, and if all those people are brought into the labor force, the pool of potential workers will grow and the price of labor will be driven down. This will encourage investment, and the economy will grow. Literacy policy is, and probably always has been, at the service of economic policy—as defined by the business community.

Some may find this view a bit too cynical, but I am reminded of this every time the unemployment rate starts to creep downward. The Federal Reserve gets worried about inflation and the possibility that wages might start to rise (God forbid!), so they raise the interest rates to put a damper on the economy and job creation. The fact is they don't want everyone to be working.

I sometimes felt the best metaphor for the whole job readiness business is a big flatbed truck driving through the neighborhood. On the truck is everyone who is working. My job is to help people get on that truck. But the truck is so full that every time I push someone up onto it, someone falls off the other side.

Of course, WIA's supporters will argue that most literacy students are coming to school because they want to be able to get a job, or if they are working they want a better job.

There is a certain limited truth to this. When we ask prospective students, in their intake interview, why they are coming back to school, many of them say some variation on the following: "I want to improve my skills so I can get my GED and get a good job." Or "So I can get my diploma and have a better life." It's clear that for most students, getting a good job is a big part of why they come. But it's also very clear that the vast, vast majority have decided that in order to do that, they need to put aside their job aspirations for the moment and develop their reading and writing skills. Moreover, to the extent that people are looking for work, that's not what they are coming to us for. In fact, people are coming to us precisely to avoid careers in low-wage (often dead-end) jobs that WIA guidelines would have us push people into.

The second point I wanted to make is that the demands of WIA, around goal setting, testing, documentation, and follow-up, at least as they are articulated in the New York State plan, are so onerous, so far removed from the realities of day-to-day life in a literacy program, that the only way to really fulfill them is to disregard our original mission. In particular, to really do the kind of follow-up called for by the Request for Proposals (RFP) would for us require hiring another full-time staff person—to handle the increased time for testing, individual goal setting, documentation, follow-up, data entry, and more.

We, of course, don't have the funds to do this. Almost lost in the discussion of goals and accountability is the dire financial situation that many programs find themselves in. We are a small program. We operate out of rented space in a commercial space in a working-class neighborhood in Brooklyn. We've struggled to maintain a stable, experienced staff and to provide them with decent working conditions. Teachers have time to talk to each other. They have time to meet with students, to do the kind of mentoring that I think is one of the hallmarks of serious education. Until this spring four out of our five teachers (counting me) plus our counselor were receiving benefits. Each year everyone on salary has received a small salary increment. However, funding, which was never adequate, has not kept up. Last year, our NYCALI budget only covered about two-thirds of our real costs, a ratio we cannot afford to maintain. Already one teacher has had to leave. We were not able to offer benefits to the person who replaced her. Now we are being asked to carry out a series of documentation, assessment, job placement, and follow-up activities without the resources to accomplish them.

What has this all meant for the classroom? Everything is being squeezed. Teacher time is devoted more and more to collecting data of dubious value, which in any case have little to do with *educational* progress. Our staff meetings have less time to talk about what is going on inside the classroom. We have had to redesign a highly individualized intake process to accommodate new testing demands.

The testing for students in the lower reading levels has presented us with special difficulties. The NYCALI RFP this year mandates that all programs offering Adult Basic Education classes use an Informal Reading Inventory (IRI) to test students in the lower reading levels. The RFP, however, didn't say which IRI we needed to use, and it was only at the Proposers' conference that we were told that we had to use the READ, a test that no one I knew had ever even seen. Now, the READ may be of some value in certain types of situations; I don't wish to argue that here. But as a standardized measure of educational gain, upon which funding decisions will apparently be based, it has no value. While the READ is designed to test a variety of word recognition and word analysis skills, the only score we are reporting (as far as I can tell, because we've had very little guidance here) is a letter grade that is determined by the student's performance in reading and answering questions about a three- or four-line paragraph.

Another demand that concerns us greatly is the requirement that 60 percent of the total number of students in the year say that their participation in the program has met their goals. How are programs going to find this out? How are we going to document it? Perhaps a short-term GED or ESL program, in which students participate for several months and then exit, could do an exit survey asking students if they had achieved their goals. But for a program like ours in which people need to make a long-term commitment to become better readers and writers, a demand like this is unrealistic. Even at our best, people drop out in the middle of the year. They may get frustrated; they may have personal problems, health crises, or family needs to attend to. For us, to meet this 60 percent level, we are going to have to find a way to continually stop and ask people, "Are you meeting your goals?"

This is not the same as asking "How can this class be improved?" "What kinds of things do you want to do next?" "How have things gone this week?" "How are you feeling about the class?" "What would you like to learn about next?" These are questions that we ask regularly and informally in the class. They are not designed to bring out yes and no answers, but thoughtful responses, in which students take increasing responsibility for the class and for their own learning. Perhaps the most upsetting thing about this 60 percent requirement is that it is not mandated by WIA, nor did it come from Washington. It came right here in New York State, perhaps in the belief that it would strengthen New York's position in acquiring funds from Washington and Albany. Whatever its purpose, it places a huge burden on already overburdened programs without leading to improved instruction.

And this is the main point, isn't it? We all need to get better at what we do. We all know that the teaching and learning at our schools can be improved. But the changes brought on by WIA, and indeed for the last several years, seem almost unconcerned with the quality of the educational program.

The beginning of the year is usually an upbeat, exciting time at the Open Book as students from last year return, re-invigorated and happy to see each other. New students come, tentative but hopeful. The talk in the classroom is full of possibilities and potentials; there is a lot of good energy. But for the teachers this year this has been overshadowed by the new era we are entering.

How are we to respond? In the face of so many, often uncertain, demands, we have tried to keep in front of us the needs of the program. We are determined to maintain as much as possible that the guiding criteria for how we design testing, intake, and follow-up procedures is what makes sense for the program.

We are determined also to play a stronger role in advocating for sensible choices in Albany and Washington. Literacy practitioners and students need a place at the table. We need to advance a vision of adult education that is aimed at meeting human needs, helping students realize their potentials, helping them learn the kinds of things they want to learn. We need to be careful about accepting things that may bring us some more money in the short run, but move us further away from a humanistic and democratic educational project. We have to acknowledge that we have in some ways been responsible for the direction WIA is taking us. Mostly, we haven't stepped up and spoken out for our vision of adult education. We have, at times, been willing to accept money even if it conflicted with our basic mission.

For me, I still consider it an honor and a privilege to be in the classroom four days a week with the incredible people who come to the Open Book. I love teaching, and most of the people I have met who do this work feel the same way. There is a sense of excitement in the classroom, a sense of being in a space with tremendous possibility, where students, many for the first time in their lives, use school to explore their own potentials as they read about and discuss the world. If we want to preserve those spaces, we're going to have to fight for them.

Bibliography

Allman, P. (1999). *Revolutionary social transformation.* Westport, CT: Bergin and Garvey.

Allman, P. (2010). *Critical education against global capitalism.* Rotterdam, Netherlands: Sense.

Aronowitz, S., and Giroux, H. (1985). *Education under siege.* South Hadley, MA: Bergin and Garvey.

Aronowitz, S., and Giroux, H. (1991). *Postmodern education: Politics, culture, and social criticism.* Minneapolis: University of Minnesota Press.

Auerbach, E. (1991). *Making meaning, making change.* Washington, DC: Center for Applied Linguistics.

Ayers, W., Hunt, J. A., and Quinn, T. (1998). *Teaching for social justice.* New York: The New Press.

Bagnall, R. (1999). *Discovering radical contingency.* New York: Peter Lang.

Bannerji, H. (2002). *Inventing subjects: Studies in hegemony, patriarchy, and colonialism.* New Delhi: Manahar Publishers.

Beder, H. (1999). *The outcomes and impacts of adult literacy education in the United States.* Cambridge, MA: National Center for the Study of Adult Learning and Literacy.

Behar, R. (1996). *The vulnerable observer.* Boston, MA: Beacon Press.

Benmayor, R. (1991). "Testimony, action research, and empowerment: Puerto Rican women and popular education." In S. B. Gluck and D. Patai (eds.), *Women's words: The feminist practice of oral history* (pp. 159–174). New York: Routledge.

Beverly, J. (2000). "Testimonio, subalternity, and narrative authority." In N. Denzin and Y. Lincoln (eds.), *Handbook of qualitative research* (pp. 555–564). Thousand Oaks, CA: Sage.

Blaise, C. (1993). *I had a father: A postmodern autobiography.* New York: HarperCollins.

Blommaert, J. (2008). *Grassroots literacy: Writing, identity, and voice in Central Africa.* London: Routledge.

Brecht, B. (1938). "The Plum Tree" [*Der Pfaumenbaum*]. From *Bertolt Brecht: Poems, 1913–1956,* p. 243. London: Methuen.

Brookfield, S. (1995). *Becoming a critically reflective teacher.* San Francisco: Jossey-Bass.

Brookfield, S. (2005). *The power of critical theory.* San Francisco: Jossey-Bass.

Calkins, L. (2000). *The art of teaching reading.* Portsmouth, NH: Heinemann.

Campbell, P., and Burnaby, B. (2001). *Participatory practices in education.* Mahwah, NJ: Lawrence Erlbaum.

Caplan, P. (1997). *African voices, African lives: Personal narratives from a Swahili village.* New York: Routledge.

Carey-Webb, A., and Benz, S. (1996). *Teaching and testimony.* Albany: State University of New York Press.

Catalfamo, A. (1998). "Opportunity or oppression." *Adult Basic Education* 8 (Spring). AAACE.

Clandin, D., and Connelly, M. (2000). *Narrative inquiry.* San Francisco: Jossey-Bass.

Cohen, D. (1998). *Radical heroes: Gramsci, Freire, and the politics of adult education.* New York: Garland.

Coles, R. (1989). *The call of stories: Teaching and the moral imaginations.* Boston: Houghton-Mifflin.

Comings, J., and Soricone, L. (2007). *Adult literacy research: Opportunities and challenges.* Cambridge, MA: National Center for the Study of Adult Learning and Literacy.

Comings, J., Garner, B., and Smith, C. (eds.). (2001). *Annual review of learning and literacy.* Volume 2. San Francisco: Jossey-Bass.

Council for Advancement of Adult Literacy (CAAL). (2002). *Research on research mini-survey.* New York: Council for Advancement of Adult Literacy.

Cunningham, P. (2000). "A sociology of adult education." In A. I. Wilson and E. R. Hayes (eds.), *Handbook of adult and continuing education* (pp. 573–588). San Francisco: Jossey-Bass.

Curtis, L. (1990). *Literacy for social change.* Syracuse, NY: New Readers Press.

Darder, A. (2003). *The critical pedagogy reader.* New York: Routledge.

De los Reyos, E., and Gozemba, P. (2002). *Pockets of hope.* Westport, CT: Bergin and Garvey.

Delpit, L. (1995). *Other people's children.* New York: W. W. Norton.

Demetrion, G. (2005). *Conflicting paradigms of adult literacy education.* Mahwah, NJ: Lawrence Erlbaum.

Division of Adult and Continuing Education. (no date). *Through the eyes of teachers: Portraits of adult students.* New York: NYS Literacy Resource Center.

Dowdy, J. (2003). *GED Stories.* New York: Peter Lang.

Dyson, M. (2007). *Debating race.* New York: Basic Books.

Ehrenreich, B. (2001). *Nickel and dimed.* New York: Owl Books.

Ellesworth, E. (1989). "Why doesn't this feel empowering: Working through the repressive myths of critical pedagogy." *Harvard Educational Review* (Fall).

Fals-Borda, O., and Rahaman, M. A. (1991). *Action and knowledge: Breaking the monopoly with participatory action-research.* New York: Apex.

Fanon, F. (1967). *Black skin, white masks.* New York: Grove Press.

Fine, M., Powell, L. C., Weis, L., and Wong, L. M. (1997). *Off white: Readings on race, power and society.* New York: Routledge.

Fine, M., Weis, L., Weseen, S., and Wong, L. (2000). "For whom?" In N. Denzin and Y. Lincoln (eds.), *Handbook of qualitative research* (pp. 107–131). Thousand Oaks, CA: Sage.

Fingeret, A., and Drennon, C. (1997). *Literacy for life.* New York: Teachers College Press.

Fontana, A., and Frey, J. (2000). "The interview: From structured questions to negotiated text." In N. Denzin and Y. Lincoln (eds.), *Handbook of qualitative research* (pp. 645–670). Thousand Oaks, CA: Sage.

Foucault, M. (1977). *Discipline and punish.* New York: Vintage.

Freire, P. (1970). *Pedagogy of the oppressed.* New York: Seabury Press.

Freire, P. (1973). *Education for critical consciousness.* New York: Continuum.

Freire, P. (1985). *The politics of education: Culture, power, and liberation.* Westport, CT: Bergin and Garvey.

Freire, P. (1995). *Pedagogy of hope: Reliving* Pedagogy of the Oppressed. New York: Continuum.

Freire, P. (1998). *Teachers as cultural workers: Letters to those who dare to teach.* Boulder, CO: Westview Press.

Freire, P., and Macedo, D. (1987). *Literacy: Reading the word and the world.* South Hadley, MA: Bergin and Garvey.

Galeano, E. (1986). *Century of the wind.* New York: W. W. Norton.

Gibbs, G. (2004). *Qualitative data analysis.* Berkshire, UK: Open University Press.

Giroux, H. (2001). *Theory and resistance in education: Towards a pedagogy for the opposition.* Westport, CT: Bergin and Garvey.

Gluck, S. B., and Patai, D. (1991). *Women's words: The feminist practice of oral history.* New York: Routledge.

Goodman, K. (1996). *On reading.* Portsmouth, NH: Heinemann.

Gordon, J. (1995). "Welfare and literacy." In *Literacy harvest.* New York: Literacy Assistance Center.

Gordon, J. (2000). "Zigs and zags of literacy: Doing literacy in the era of WIA." Unpublished article.

Greene, M. (1997). *A light in dark times: Maxine Greene and the unfinished conversation.* New York: Teachers College Press.

Guy, T. (ed.). (1999). *Providing culturally relevant education.* New directions for adult and continuing education. No. 82. San Francisco: Jossey-Bass.

Hansman, C., and Sissel, P. (eds.). (2001). *Understanding and negotiating the political landscape of adult education.* New directions for adult and continuing education. No. 91. San Francisco: Jossey-Bass.

Hart, M. (2001). "Transforming boundaries of power in the classroom: Learning from la mestiza." In R. Cevero and A. Wilson (eds.), *Power in practice* (pp. 164–183). San Francisco: Jossey-Bass.

Heaney, T. (1996). *Adult education for social change: From center stage to the wings and back again.* Washington, DC: Office of Educational Research and Improvement. (ERIC Document Reproduction Service No. ED 396190).

Heaney, T. (2000). "Adult education and society." In A. I. Wilson and E. R. Hayes (eds.), *Handbook of adult and continuing education* (pp. 559–570). San Francisco: Jossey-Bass.

Heath, S. (1983). *Ways with words: Language, life, and work in communities and classrooms.* Cambridge, UK: Cambridge University Press.

Hemphill, D. (2001). "Incorporating postmodernist perspectives in adult education." In P. Sissel and V. Sheared (eds.), *Making space.* Westport, CT: Bergin and Garvey.

Holstein, J., and Gubrium, J. (1995). *The active interview.* Thousand Oaks, CA: Sage.

hooks, b. (1994). *Teaching to transgress.* London, UK: Routledge.

Hord, F., and Lee, J. (1995). *I am because we are: Readings in black philosophy.* Amherst: University of Massachusetts Press.

Horseman, J. (1990). *Something in my mind besides the everyday.* Toronto: Canadian Scholars Press.

Horton, M., and Freire, P. (1990). *We make the road by walking.* Philadelphia: Temple University Press.

Horton, M., Kohl, J., and Kohl, H. (1998). *The long haul.* New York: Teachers College Press.

Hoyles, M. (ed.). (1977). *The politics of literacy.* London: Writers and Readers Cooperative Society.

Hughes, L. (1994). *The collected poems of Langston Hughes.* New York: Alfred Knopf.

Hull, G. (ed.). (1997). *Changing work, changing workers.* Albany: State University of New York Press.

Johnson-Bailey, J. (2004). *Sistahs in college.* Malabar, FL: Krieger.

Kemmis, S., and McTaggart, R. (2000). "Participatory action research." In N. Denzin and Y. Lincoln (eds.), *Handbook of qualitative research* (pp. 567–605). Thousand Oaks, CA: Sage.

Kim, K., Hagedorn, M., Williamson, J., and Chapman, C. (2004). "Participation in adult education and lifelong learning: 2000–01." *National Household Education Surveys of 2001.* Washington, DC: U.S. Department of Education.

Kincheloe, J. L., and Steinberg, S. R. (1998). *Unauthorized methods: Strategies for critical teaching.* New York: Routledge.

Kingfisher, C. P. (1996). *Women in the American welfare trap.* Philadelphia: University of Pennsylvania Press.

Kozol, J. (1992). *Savage inequalities.* New York: Crown Publishers.

Kucer, S. (2001). *Dimensions of literacy.* Mahwah, NJ: Lawrence Erlbaum.

Lather, P. (1991). *Getting smart.* New York: Routledge.

Lindeman, E. (1961). *The meaning of adult education.* Norman: Oklahoma Research Center for Continuing Professional and Higher Education.

Luttrell, W. (1997). *School-smart and mother-wise.* New York: Routledge.

Mace, J. (1992). *Talking about literacy.* London, UK: Routledge.

Macedo, D. (1994). *Literacies of power: What Americans are not allowed to know.* Boulder, CO: Westview Press.

Maguire, P. (1987). *Doing participatory research: A feminist approach.* Amherst: University of Massachusetts Press.

Martin, R. (2001). *Listening up.* Portsmouth, NH: Heinemann.

Mayo, P. (1999). *Gramsci, Freire, and adult education.* London: Zed Books.

McLaren, P. (1998). *Life in schools: An introduction to critical pedagogy in the foundations of education,* 3rd ed. New York: Longman.

McLaren, P., and Leonard, P. (eds.). (1993). *Paulo Freire: A critical encounter.* London: Routledge.

Memmi, A. (1965). *The colonizer and the colonized.* Boston, MA: Beacon Press.

Menchu, R. (1983). *I, Rigoberta Menchú.* London, UK: New Left Books.

Merriam, S., and Simpson, E. (2000). *A guide to research for educators and trainers of adults.* Melbourne, FL: Krieger.

Merrifield, J., Bingman, M., Hemphill, D., and Bennet de Marrais, K. (1997). *Life at the margins.* New York: Teachers College Press.

Morgan, B. (1998). *The ESL classroom.* Toronto: University of Toronto Press.

Morley, D., and Worpole, K. (2010). *The republic of letters: Working-class writing and local publishing.* Syracuse, NY: University of Syracuse Press.

Morris, A. (1984). *The origins of the civil rights movement.* New York: Free Press.

Morrow, R. A., and Torres, C. A. (1995). *Social theory and education: A critique of theories of social and cultural reproduction.* New York: State University of New York Press.

Nadeau, D. (1996). "Embodying feminist popular education under global restructuring." In S. Walters and L. Manicom (eds.), *Gender and popular education* (pp. 40–60). Atlantic Highlands, NJ: Zed Books.

National Assessment of Adult Literacy (2003). Retrieved from http://nces.ed.gov/NAAL/index.

National Institute for Literacy (NIFL). (2002). Literacy skills for the 21st century America. Retrieved from http://www.nifl.gov/summit.

Nesbit, T. (2004). "Class and teaching." In R. St. Clair and J. Sandlin (eds.), *Promoting critical practice in adult education.* New Directions for Adult and Continuing Education. No. 102. San Francisco: Jossey-Bass, 2004.

Ornelas, A. (1997). "Pasantias and social participation: Participatory action research as a way of life." In S. Smith, D. Willms, and N. Johnson (eds.), *Nurtured by knowledge.* New York: Apex.

Park, P., Brydon-Miller, M., Hall, B., and Jackson, T. (1993). *Voices of change: Participatory research in the United States and Canada.* Toronto: OISIE Press.

Portelli, A. (1998). "What makes oral history different." In R. Perks and A. Thomson (eds.), *The oral history reader* (pp. 53–62). New York: Routledge.

Prins, E., Toso, B., and Schafft, K. (2008). *The importance of social interaction and support for women learners: Evidence from family literacy programs.* University Park, PA: Goodling Institute for Research in Family Literacy.

Purcell-Gates, V., and Waterman, R. (2000). *Now we read, we see, we speak.* Mahwah, NJ: Lawrence Erlbaum.

Quigley, A. (1997). *Rethinking literacy education.* San Francisco, CA: Jossey-Bass.

Ramdeholl, D. (2007). "It must be told:Stories of dreams, hope, and possibility from the Open Book." Paper presented at the 48th Adult Education Research Conference. Halifax, Nova Scotia: Mount Saint Vincent University.

Rich, A. (1994). *Blood, bread, and poetry: Selected prose, 1979–1985.* New York: W. W. Norton.

Riessman, C. (2003). *Narrative analysis.* Newbury Park, CA: Sage.

Rivera, R. (2008). *Laboring to learn: Women's literacy and poverty in the post-welfare era.* Urbana: University of Illinois Press.

Rose, M. (1989). *Lives on the boundary.* New York: Penguin.

Ruiz, A. (1989). *Four stories: Oral histories of the Open Book.* New York: Open Book.

Sandlin, J. (2004). "Designing women: Gender and power in welfare-to-work educational programs." In M. Miller (ed.), *Women and literacy: Moving to power and participation* (pp. 147–162). New York: Feminist Press.

Sangster, J. (1998). "Telling our stories: Feminist debates and the use of oral history." In R. Perks and A. Thomson (eds.), *The oral history reader* (pp. 87–99). New York: Routledge.

Shor, I. (1980). *Critical teaching and everyday life.* Chicago: University of Chicago Press.

Shor, I. (1987). *Freire for the classroom.* Portsmouth, NH: Heinemann.

Shor, I. (1992). *Empowering education.* Chicago: University of Chicago Press.

Sissel, P. (1996). *A community based approach to literacy programs: Taking learners' lives into account.* San Francisco: Jossey-Bass.

Sissel, P., and Sheared, V. (2001). *Making space.* Westport, CT: Bergin and Garvey.

Slim, H., and Thompson, P. (1995). *Listening for a change.* Philadelphia, PA: New Society Publishers.

Smith, S., Willms, D., and Johnson, N. (eds.). (1997). *Nurtured by knowledge.* New York: Apex.

Sparks, B., and Peterson, E. (2000). "Adult basic education and the crisis of accountability." In A. I. Wilson and E. R. Hayes (eds.), *Handbook of adult and continuing education* (pp. 263–275). San Francisco: Jossey-Bass.

St. Clair, R., and Sandlin, J. (eds.). (2004). *Promoting critical practice in adult education.* New Directions for Adult and Continuing Education. No. 102. San Francisco: Jossey-Bass.

Stuckey, E. J. (1991). *The violence of literacy.* Portsmouth, NH: Heinemann.

Students and Staff of the Open Book. (1991). *We're all in this together: Leadership and community at the Open Book.* Brooklyn, NY: Self-published.

Thompson, P. (1998). "The voice of the past: Oral history." In R. Perks and A. Thomson (eds.), *The oral history reader* (pp. 21–28). New York: Routledge.

Thompson, P. (2000). *The voice from the past.* Oxford: Oxford University Press.

Tierney, W. G., and Lincoln, Y. S. (1997). *Representation and the text: Re-framing the narrative voice.* Albany: State University of New York Press.

Torres, C. A. (1995). "Participatory action research and popular education in Latin America." In P. McLaren and J. Giarelli (eds.), *Critical theory and educational research.* Albany: State University of New York Press.

Tyler, D. (1997). *Many families, many literacies.* Portsmouth, NH: Heinemann.

Underwood, P. (1994). *Winter white and summer gold: A Native American learning story.* Bayfield, CO: Tribe of Two Press.

United States Census Bureau (2008). "Educational attainment: American Community Survey." Retrieved from www.factfinder.census.gov.

United States Department of Education, National Center for Education Statistics (2002). "Participation trends and patterns in adult education: 1991–1999." NCES 2002-119, by S. Creighton and L. Hudson. Washington, DC: Office of Educational Research and Improvement, U.S. Department of Education.

Usher, R., Bryant, I., and Johnston, R. (1997). *Adult education and the postmodern challenge.* London: Routledge.

Vaz, K. M. (1997). *Oral narrative research with black women.* Thousand Oaks, CA: Sage.

Wasserman, P. (2000). "Leadership in an era of change." In *Literacy harvest.* New York: The Literacy Assistance Center.

Weiler, K. (1988). *Women teaching for change: Gender, class, and power.* South Hadley, MA: Bergin and Garvey.

Worpole, K. (1977). "Beyond the classroom walls." In M. Hoyles (ed.), *The politics of literacy.* London: Writers and Readers Cooperative Society.

About the Author

Dianne Ramdeholl is Assistant Professor of Educational Studies at the School for Graduate Studies at Empire State College. She has been an adult literacy worker and advocate for improving quality of adult literacy education. Her principal focus research has been developing educational projects that promote equitable socioeconomic conditions and that connect disenfranchised populations to increased participation in democratic decision-making.